Social Media Marketing

An Essential Guide to Building a Brand Using Facebook, YouTube, Instagram, Snapchat, and Twitter, Including Tips on Personal Branding, Advertising and Using Influencers

Contents

INTRODUCTION 1

CHAPTER 1: WHY IS SOCIAL MEDIA (STILL) IMPORTANT? 3

CONNECTING TO POTENTIAL CUSTOMERS.. 4

IMPROVING YOUR REPUTATION 4

SOCIAL MEDIA MARKETING 5

IMPROVING YOUR SEO.. 5

CUSTOMER REVIEWS... 6

BUILDING RELATIONSHIPS WITH YOUR CUSTOMERS........................ 7

SOCIAL MEDIA IS PLAYFUL AND FUN... 7

BOOSTING SALES.. 8

COLLABORATING WITH OTHER ORGANIZATIONS............................... 8

CHAPTER 2: CHANGES TO EXPECT IN 2020 10

CHANGES TO EXPECT ACROSS ALL SOCIAL MEDIA PLATFORMS 11

INCREASED PRIVACY 12

FOCUS ON IMPROVED ALGORITHMS.. 12

USING ARTIFICIAL INTELLIGENCE TO FILTER OUT FAKE NEWS 13

CHANGES TO EXPECT FROM SPECIFIC PLATFORMS 13

INSTAGRAM 13

FACEBOOK 14

YOUTUBE 15

SNAPCHAT 15

TWITTER 16

CHAPTER 3: SOCIAL MEDIA TRENDS FOR 2020 18

TREND 1: POWERFUL STORYTELLING 18

TREND 2: VIDEO CONTENT AND ENGAGEMENT 20

TREND 3: RISE OF INFLUENCER MARKETING 20

TREND 4: STORIES AND IGTV VIDEOS 21

TREND 5: INCREASE IN SHOPPING 22

TREND 6: INCORPORATION OF AUGMENTED REALITY FOR CUSTOMERS ... 23

CHAPTER 4: PERSONAL BRANDING—ARE YOU DOING IT RIGHT?
.... **25**

PRODUCT BRANDING 25

PERSONAL BRANDING 26

CLEAN OUT YOUR SOCIAL MEDIA PLATFORMS 26

BE CONSISTENT 27

MAINTAIN A VISUALLY APPEALING FRONT 27

FIND THE MOST SUITABLE PLATFORM FOR YOUR BUSINESS 28

ANALYZE YOUR AUDIENCE 28

CHOOSE OTHER BRAND AMBASSADORS 28

BE ACTIVE ON SOCIAL MEDIA 29

VIDEO CONTENT 31

CHAPTER 5: KNOWING AND GROWING YOUR AUDIENCE 32

PINPOINTING YOUR AUDIENCE 32

CHARACTERISTICS TO HELP YOU DEFINE YOUR AUDIENCE 33

GROWING YOUR AUDIENCE 35

CHAPTER 6: WHICH PLATFORM SHOULD YOU USE? 38

FACEBOOK 38

INSTAGRAM 39

SNAPCHAT 40

TWITTER 40

YOUTUBE 41

TIKTOK 42

LINKEDIN 42

PINTEREST 43

CHAPTER 7: FACEBOOK MARKETING **45**

STRATEGY 1: ENGAGING CONTENT 45

STRATEGY 2: VIDEO CONTENT 47

STRATEGY 3: FACEBOOK ADS... 51

TYPES OF FACEBOOK ADS 51

HOW TO ADVERTISE ON FACEBOOK 53

CHAPTER 8: YOUTUBE MARKETING **56**

STRATEGY 1: OPTIMIZED CONTENT 57

TYPE OF CONTENT... 57

PRACTICE CONSISTENCY... 58

USE SEO FOR VIDEO TITLES AND DESCRIPTIONS.................... 59

STRATEGY 2: YOUTUBE STORIES.. 59

BENEFITS OF USING YOUTUBE STORIES 60

WHAT DOES ITS FUTURE LOOK LIKE? 62

STRATEGY 3: YOUTUBE ADVERTISING................................... 63

TYPES OF YOUTUBE ADS.. 63

CHAPTER 9: TWITTER MARKETING **65**

SETTING TARGETS AND AN ULTIMATE GOAL 66

FOUR GREAT WAYS OF PLANNING 67

STRATEGY 1: PERSONALIZED RESPONSES............................... 69

STRATEGY 2: PROPER HASHTAG USE 70

STRATEGY 3: THE USE OF VISUALS....................................... 71

A FEW MORE TIPS... 72

CHAPTER 10: INSTAGRAM MARKETING **74**

STRATEGY 1: INSTAGRAM STORIES 75

Other Tips 77

Strategy 2: Shopping Posts..77

Why is Instagram Shopping a Great Marketing Tool? 78

Setting up Instagram Shopping..79

Strategy 3: Instagram Ads..80

CHAPTER 11: SNAPCHAT MARKETING 83

Why Snapchat? 84

Reasons to Include Snapchat in Your Marketing Plan 84

Strategy 1: Linked Stories..85

Strategy 2: Behind-the-Scenes Snaps................................86

How to Use Behind-the-Scenes Content on Snapchat 87

Strategy 3: Snapchat Ads 87

Types of Ads 88

Snapchat Ads Manager..89

Additional Tips..90

CHAPTER 12: THE RISE OF INFLUENCER MARKETING AND HOW TO USE IT..92

Why Is Influencer Marketing on the Rise?................................92

How Does a Business Use Influencer Marketing? 93

What Can an Influencer Do for Your Business? 94

Review Your Products or Services 94

Give your Business a Shout-Out 95

Take Over Your Account 95

Benefitting from Micro-Influencers................................96

CHAPTER 13: TOP 7 SOCIAL MEDIA TOOLS FOR 2020......99

1. TubeBuddy 99

2. Keywords Everywhere 101

3. Flume..101

4. Later 102

5. Your Analytics 103

6. Anchor..104

7. Quora..104

CHAPTER 14: THE FUTURE OF SOCIAL MEDIA MARKETING 106

FOCUS ON USER ENGAGEMENT.. 106

BUILD RELATIONSHIPS 107

CREATE YOUR OWN INFLUENCERS 107

CAPITALIZE ON OMNICHANNEL MARKETING............................ 108

CONCENTRATE ON CONTENT MARKETING 108

USE USER METRICS TO BEAT GOOGLE 109

REMEMBER THE IMPORTANCE OF BRANDING............................ 110

DON'T RESTRICT YOURSELF TO CONVENTIONAL TRAFFIC METHODS.... 110

THINK LIKE A WINNER.. 111

CONCLUSION 112

RESOURCES..113

Introduction

You know why you are here. You're aware of the importance of social media marketing and its potential in 2020, and want to use this amazing tool to strategize content for brand recognition and more sales. But how exactly do you do that, and where do you start?

In this book, you will find up-to-date tips and tricks, along with expert strategies that will help your brand make its mark across social media platforms this year. Even though it contains a few advanced approaches, it is a straightforward read that'll help you maneuver through the hardest gimmicks effortlessly.

Any business today turns to social media to accelerate their performance and engage more customers, which is wise. But there is so much going on with social media platforms right now—like the introduction of new features every year, brands using maximum creativity to engage their followers, and the rise of new companies and influencers carving their niche—that it can feel overwhelming to try and stand out in such a saturated market. This is where this book will come to your rescue. Every page consists of well-versed tactics that will change the way you interact with your customers, helping you create a brand image that you would otherwise not have imagined.

If you are just starting out—or simply thinking of starting out—with social media marketing, you might not know the importance of these platforms. You might also have asked yourself, "Is social media really important for my business?" The answer to this question is always, "Yes!" Social media marketing is necessary for every discipline thriving today. On the other hand, if you're a prominent marketer or an entrepreneur who is familiar with the world of social media, you already know that the majority of your customers use it, and it offers you the opportunity of generating more sales. So, why not use these free tools to your advantage?

Social media can provide you and your brand with several benefits, some of which include building a brand image, spreading your brand's products and principles across the world, unlocking your creative potential, offering better customer service, showing your brand's authenticity, and building your presence in today's digital world. Your website and social media accounts are the first things that your customers are going to check before trusting your products and services, and you have landed on the right book to help you create that great first online impression.

It is time to take social media more seriously and think of it as more than just a fad. No wonder there are specialized courses on it, and job openings that request social media managers and strategists to take over a company's social media department. This book will help you gain insight into many professional tips that will allow you to handle your brand's social media marketing by yourself without having to hire expert teams. By using this blank canvas, you can create your own community or cult and follow your own style while doing so. It guides you through the challenges of presenting the best content you have to offer.

Read on to excel in social media marketing and brand building in 2020, with this thorough blueprint for success.

Chapter 1: Why Is Social Media (Still) Important?

On any given day, at any given time, you will always find people staring at their phones, scrolling through social media. Social media has become a virtual world for each person to escape into, and they get to customize it according to the people and pages they choose to follow. So, if you are asking why social media is important, here are a few facts to set the record straight.

Why social media? Well, because the use of social media around the world is constantly on the rise. Since 2004, the number of users has increased every year, making it an easy resource that needs to be taken advantage of. You would be surprised to know that, in 2019, the number of Internet users spiked by a whopping 9.1 percent to a total of 4.388 billion users. Can you imagine having all these people at reach and not trying to make the most of it for your business? Not only that but of those Internet users, 3.484 billion were on social media 9 percent more than they were the year before. One of the main reasons why social media is so accessible is because smartphones have made it possible for people to access any application with just a click of a button.

So, the next question to ask here is: *How can social media be beneficial for a business?* Well, read on to learn about the advantages of using social media for professional purposes.

Connecting to Potential Customers

One of the best ways to familiarize customers with your company and what it has to offer is through social media. With many people using social media daily, it is easier to target your customers and reach them where they are most likely to be; on their social media platforms. An average person spends at least two hours and 22 minutes per day on social networks, scrolling through their feed, messaging their friends, and trying to post the perfect breakfast photo.

Because of the amount of time spent on social media, it has become a vital resource to capitalize on in order to reach the right audience. Depending on your target audience and what product or service your company offers, the importance of each platform will differ in finding potential customers. However, to maintain a strong image, you must have a strong online presence, which leads to the next point.

Improving Your Reputation

Imagine scrolling through your feed, and a sponsored post of something you are actually interested in comes up. What is the first thing you do? Click on the post and take a glance at the account, of course. In that split second, the number of followers your business account has will have a strong impact on whether or not the user will continue to scroll through your feed.

Unfortunately, social media has given users the ability to judge a book by its cover—in this case, the number of followers and posts, the amount of interaction, and the overall appearance of your social media account. These will instantly be an indication of how legitimate your business is and whether it is worth taking the time to check out the feed or not. It's sad that it's come to this, but it is what it is, and as a business owner, you need to ensure that your online presence is a good indication of your reputable business. You should make sure that your online presence is strong enough to make potential customers stay.

Social Media Marketing

Is social media marketing still a thing? Yes, it is! And it's still as effective as ever. However, before investing in social media marketing, you need to familiarize yourself with two things: understanding the algorithm of the platform you are using to advertise and optimizing the tools to your advantage by targeting the audience correctly to reach the demographics, age, gender, and other specifications you can use to filter your audience.

With social media marketing, you will be able to reach a wider range of users with better stakes, as it is more targeted and directed at actual users who seem to fit the right profile. Not only that, but it's also a cheaper medium as you manage to allocate a very small budget per post instead of spending hefty sums on other forms of marketing and advertisement. In the following chapters, you will be provided with a detailed explanation of how to use each social media platform to your advantage, and which platform will be more suitable for your business type.

Improving Your SEO

Optimizing your SEO is important to give your business the possibility of being seen on the first couple of pages of a Google search. Using the right keywords on your website is just one way to optimize your SEO ranking on Google and make your website or social media platforms more visible. However, another way to gain advantage and direct more traffic to your website is by using social media. Because SEO ranking also factors in usability and the engagement that takes place on your company's social platforms, it recognizes engagement as an indication of your business's reliability, giving it a further push in terms of SEO.

The more present you are on social media, the more likely it is to grab a potential customer's attention and have that potential customer head to your company's website or profile to find out more. This not only gets you more clicks on your website—increasing the SEO ranking—but also paves the way for your customers to reach your products or services and takes them one step closer to making a purchase. That is why it is essential to make your content relatable, engaging, and appealing to your target audience, while always optimizing the necessary keywords to boost your SEO and make your business easier for new customers to find.

Customer Reviews

While some people view a business' social media accounts to get an idea of what they have to offer, others use them to get feedback in terms of the business's products or services. Social media has made it easier for people to voice their opinions without feeling embarrassed, as it is not done in person but through a virtual platform where you never have to meet the people that you are criticizing or praising.

Say a potential customer comes across your products and is interested in buying them; instead of making deciding on a whim, it is quite likely that they will visit your social media platforms and see if any customers have left reviews, or even scroll through your posts to check if there are any negative or positive comments from previous users. The feedback they encounter will gravely affect their decision; it will either help remove the doubts and skepticism they have and encourage them to make a purchase, or put them off entirely and make you lose a customer for good. That is why it is imperative that you handle customer feedback with care and always ensure that your business responds to any negative feedback with professionalism. You need to handle the situation as wisely as possible to prevent it from having an impact on other customers and ruining the reputation of your business. Remember that customer feedback is a double-edged sword that has the power to make or break your reputation and affect your business accordingly.

Building Relationships with Your Customers

Being active on social media allows your customers to get a better understanding of your identity, not only through the products or services you offer but also the tone of voice you use. This helps them relate to your business more and therefore becomes more interactive. When a customer sees your posts frequently and interacts with them regularly, a virtual relationship is formed, making their connection to your brand stronger. Using this concept to your advantage will help you generate better content on social media and allow you to get to know your clients on a personal level.

Social media gives you the ability to monitor and analyze what resonates with the customers and helps you improve your products, services, and social media posts to suit their tastes. The more appealing the content, the stronger the relationship with your customers. In turn, you will be able to have insight into their interests, characters, and what they are drawn to. You'll also realize that as the bond gets stronger, the customer's sense of loyalty toward your brand will increase, making them more inclined to stick with your products instead of those of your competitors.

Social Media is Playful and Fun

There is so much to do on social media besides posting pictures and videos. You can launch interactive social media campaigns—giving your audience a chance to engage in creating videos, take quizzes, or shoot creative photographs of themselves using your products. This not only gives your audience the chance to get creative and enjoy themselves through your brand but also helps them promote your business through their own social media channels as they tag their friends or post whatever they have created on their platforms.

With social media, you have the freedom to try out different mediums, making your brand get identified as fun, interactive, and enjoyable to follow. It also allows you to be timely and use trending topics to your advantage in a playful way that makes your brand even more appealing to your audience. Besides, allowing people to engage with your content in order to get a reward is a great, cheap marketing option that is extremely easy and effective, thanks to social media.

Boosting Sales

If you want to boost your sales, it is not enough to just have a website. Using social media can really help generate more sales as it tends to humanize your brand and increase brand loyalty, as well as reach a wider audience. Instead of having customers come to you, social media allows you to penetrate their feeds. As users scroll through their feeds and see your business's posts, they are constantly reminded of the products or services you offer, keeping your brand on their minds. This allows them to accumulate more knowledge about your brand and products, and easily recommend it to those around them when asked about a company that provides your services. The more exposure your business gets on social media, the higher the number of sales you will generate.

Collaborating with Other Organizations

Because everyone is connected on social media, it makes it fairly easy for your business to reach out to potential companies you feel are a good match and join forces in a collaboration to bring something innovative, exciting, and new to your customers. Not only that, but you can also gain access to a completely different target audience—or reach a wider one—by collaborating with social media influencers and having them promote your brand or engage in a specific campaign.

There are so many ways that social media can be beneficial for business purposes. This makes it not only useful but imperative for a company to have a strong social media presence and really put effort into capitalizing on social media marketing. It is an easy, effective tool that requires minimal resources and generates excellent results, as well as detailed information and analysis to help ensure that your business is moving in the right direction according to what the market needs.

Chapter 2: Changes to Expect in 2020

While the past decade has witnessed a phenomenal rise in social media usage and heavy traffic, content marketers and agencies are rapidly gaining benefits from it. Social media was merely used for entertainment and sharing users' favorite moments in the beginning, but it has now become a major business tool for companies in almost all disciplines. A chunk of the world population has made social media their full-time job, making millions out of creating and sharing content.

Aside from various employment opportunities, social media platforms are also giving people a chance to showcase their talent to the world. Companies are now making sales through social media like never before. And this is only going to increase this year and beyond—so much so that companies are hiring social media managers and content marketers just to handle their social media platforms. While the millennials are already hitting the bullseye, Gen Z is ready to take over the commercial discipline, adding to the inventiveness and originality of social media marketing facets across various platforms.

In 2020, social media will continue to flourish, although many changes are expected. You, too, can benefit from these. This chapter will focus on all the changes that might occur this year, some of which can be directed entirely toward increasing engagement. The year 2017 witnessed a massive growth in social media users, with around one million people joining various platforms every day, and it does not seem to be stopping anytime soon. With this increasing engagement, social media platforms, such as Facebook, Instagram, YouTube, Snapchat, and Twitter, are rapidly experimenting with specific technical changes that can improve user experience. These changes are also being implemented due to privacy breaches, an increase in fake accounts, hackers, and the transmission of fake news.

You need to be aware of these algorithm changes, as they can significantly affect your marketing process.

Changes to Expect Across All Social Media Platforms

Social media can collectively experience some changes this year, with some of the platforms making a few standard modifications. This will not only affect the habits of users but also massively change marketing strategies and business approaches.

Everyone saw Instagram and Facebook adding the feature of stories a few years ago, taking over Snapchat's entire engagement concept, which has now become a big-time engagement tactic for increasing followers and likes. This is because stories were developed for easy access, uplifting the user's experience. Stories are temporarily produced, visually interactive content, and it is easy for users to view the enlarged content without having to rotate the phone. These aspects are mainly what made stories a major hit as a feature. And so, many bloggers use them as a creative way of storytelling, keeping their followers engaged.

This is a good example of how social media platforms are realizing the importance of user mindset and suggesting a few feature changes by implementing several technological advancements and artificial intelligence.

Increased Privacy

The use of social media has exposed people's personal lives to the public, which can be threatening. With the recent Facebook data breach accusations, the social media platform is on its way toward developing a more secure and private network, which can be expected by the end of this year. Not only Facebook, but many leading platforms are alarmed and cautious about increasing privacy to generate better numbers and ratings. When you sign up for any social media platform, you need to fill in general information that is being stored by the respective companies. While this cannot be entirely avoided, people are keen to know the steps these giants are taking to promise better security. This will not only establish brand trust but also induce a feeling of enhanced regulations for the people who are currently on major channels.

Focus on Improved Algorithms

For any social media platform to be successful, the artificial intelligence algorithm needs to align with the human algorithm that is the user experience and the intent. It is basically what a human expects and accordingly fetches possibilities from the platform. Instead of thinking computing, tech giants are designing their algorithms to make them more human-centered and relevant. Even if accounts lose engagement on individual posts, they might still gain more followers and promise an overall better user experience. If this change is implemented rapidly, this might affect your audience engagement. In this case, you will have to follow tactics that will hold your audience's interest and acknowledge individual posts for creativity and originality, while getting familiar with the concept of a human algorithm to reach your desired audience and get more followers.

Using Artificial Intelligence to Filter Out Fake News

One of the main reasons why users do not usually trust social media platforms for current affairs and up-to-date information is the spread of fake news. False information can significantly affect people's sense of perception, and that is why social media giants and developers are relying on artificial intelligence to filter out fake news and segment data to present accurate and reliable information. With an unfathomable amount of content created and posted on social media, people need a utilitarian artificial intelligence system within the algorithm to crack the complex data and clean it for legitimate results.

Changes to Expect from Specific Platforms

Here is how individual social media channels are experimenting with changes and adding features, some of which can be put into use in 2020:

Instagram

● **Hiding the Likes**
Instagram has been testing this new feature of hiding likes from posts in countries such as Italy, Australia, Ireland, and Japan since the year 2019. While hackers and bots are slowly creeping in to increase fake followers and likes, companies and creators who produce genuine content are affected. Also, the new generation is highly affected by the number of likes garnered by their posts and content, which forces them to compare. Eventually, the result is disappointment and self-doubt. To make the user experience more authentic, Instagram is working on hiding likes from posts. You, as the owner of your account and content, can view the number of likes. Depending on the type of discipline you are in, this may or may not affect your marketing strategies. For instance, if you're an entrepreneur, you will need to focus more on your number of followers than your likes. But if you're

an influencer, your work and content generation might get somewhat affected.

- **Enhanced Business Tools**

Even though Instagram has massively improved its business tools feature in the past few years, there might be bigger and better changes this year. Many companies are handling business through Instagram now, which is likely why you are here, too. Switching to a business account instead of a personal one gives you additional benefits like insight into user engagement, audience interaction with individual posts, and direct contact with potential customers. This year, you might see improved customer service and tweaked insight statistics, helping you to generate more revenue.

Facebook

• Focus on Groups

Facebook has been working on improving its groups feature for enhanced user experience since 2017. With useful add-ins such as watch party and Facebook pixel, users were able to revamp their content engagement experience. A few additions and design changes made in 2019 also proved to be successful. They drove more people to use this augmented feature and increased interaction. This year, expect a further boost in the groups tab that will pique users' interest, helping your business grow through social media.

• Cryptocurrency and Facebook Pay

Facebook is all set to launch Calibra, its dedicated wallet, to introduce its own global payment system. Facebook's digital currency is called Libra, and it aims to change and dominate the payment discipline around the world. It is designed to be used for normal transactions like paying grocery bills as well, without any transaction costs. Calibra will be integrated into Facebook, Messenger, and WhatsApp. This will majorly affect your methods of carrying out business transactions.

YouTube

- **Ads You Cannot Skip**

Even though people are currently witnessing this feature that was added at the beginning of 2019, YouTube is aiming to extend this practice because more people are using the application on their smart TVs. This can elevate your streaming experience and give you opportunities to present your content to a bigger audience. With the addition of the TrueView ad unit, you can seamlessly incorporate creativity that was initially targeted to TV viewers.

- **Creation of Original Content**

People have seen YouTube rolling out original content with its own series and live events being streamed on the platform. While there is no Premium paywall on it anymore, the platform might invest more in producing this kind of original content this year. It is also produced with versatility and diversity in mind. It marks the importance of content originality, especially advertisements. You really need to focus on this aspect if you are planning on using YouTube as one of your primary platforms for marketing.

Snapchat

- **Enhanced AR Filters**

Augmented reality is booming in this technology-driven era, with social media platforms keen on passing the experience on to their users. Snapchat has always been—and probably will be—the leading platform to use this tool. With creative tools, interactive templates, and the use of geolocation, Snapchat makes people think, "What's next?"

The platform recently shook hands with a computer vision startup, AI Factory, which will help in enhancing existing features and creating plausible interactive tools. Also, you can expect some goofy AR filters that will probably go viral.

- **Ad Tools**

Snapchat is really stepping up its ad game with the recent introduction of Dynamic Ads. It is still experimenting with updated formats that can be released this year. The feature of Dynamic Ads can be extremely helpful for marketers and content creators trying to sell products or services. These are tweaked to change particular product information and present it in its most creative and truest form. You can choose from a wide range of templates available that work as complete product catalogs for all disciplines and have been successful in catching users' attention. With better ad experiences expected this year, you can fully benefit from this feature by targeting younger users, as they constitute the majority of users.

Twitter

•Switching Accounts in Replies

A probable feature rolling out this year could be the ability to switch accounts while you are replying to a tweet. This could help in replying to potential clients, using both your accounts spontaneously. While this feature was merely an experiment, it is likely to be made permanent this year.

- **Tweeting to Specific Topics or Friends**

Dantley Davis, the vice president of Twitter's design and research department, recently displayed a list of probable features that could be introduced this year. One of the main highlights was the feature of tweeting to specific subjects, friends, or hashtags. This will allow you to tweet on specific subjects or promote your business in segments by using particular hashtags or targeting your audience group. It is aimed at preventing spamming and targeting users who are truly curious. However, it may also open up the potential of forming private discussions or groups, similar to Facebook. In that case, you will have to channel your strategies in the right direction wisely.

As you can see, many of these foreseeable changes across all social media platforms can benefit your marketing strategies, while a few of them need to be molded and targeted to your advantage. Improved features like refined customer service, more ads across all platforms, and enhanced business and interaction tools can make your business marketing stronger than ever.

Chapter 3: Social Media Trends for 2020

As you start thinking that social media has reached its peak, it tends to do better and prove you wrong. The last five to seven years have witnessed a drastic growth in social media use, with marketers and brands making all these platforms their main base for advertising. If you are just entering this game now, you need to stay ahead of time. While you're already aware of the changes that might occur in social media this year, here are some of the trends that you must follow to stand out and generate more leads.

Trend 1: Powerful Storytelling

The power of authentic advertising was revealed in this past decade, with agencies and brands creating content that oozed creativity and originality. People can anticipate how audiences can be attracted to advertising and marketing that is pure genius.

Here is how you can grab your audience's attention with some remarkable and powerful storytelling:

Personalization

You know your story will hit the mark when the majority of your audience can relate to it. Although considered an underrated tactic, personalization can actually be a game-changer for you. Many marketers are now realizing this and actively using it within their phases of marketing strategies. It not only helps your audience to make a wiser purchase decision but also leaves a great impression on them. You might have noticed how Spotify rolled out personalized statistics for every user at the end of 2019. This was an amazing way to generate more interaction, and Spotify was thoroughly successful in achieving it.

Hitting the Current Affairs

Staying up to date with current news and using it to your advantage is another underrated yet powerful strategy that can be used in a scholarly marketing plan. One great example of a brand that follows smart advertising and uses powerful storytelling, mainly through current affairs, is Burger King. A recent piece of news about Prince Harry and Meghan Markle stepping back from their senior royal roles was seen as a great marketing tactic by the brand. They instantly tweeted, "@ harry, this royal family offers part-time positions" and "You can still eat like a king with us, Harry." While some followers appreciated Burger King for their brilliant timing, others criticized the brand for crossing the line. In both cases, they got enough publicity by gathering more audience engagement that eventually helped their business.

Using Humor

Audiences of all ages can relate to comedy and humor, depending on its context and subject. It is high time you understood the value of humor, too; you can actively use it this year within your content. Two brands that have taken over Twitter and Facebook with their humorous one-liners, clever photo uploads, and witty comebacks are Taco Bell and Old Spice. A recent tiff between Taco Bell and Old Spice on Twitter interested their audiences and significantly increased their engagement. Using humor shows that your brand is authentic, human, and relevant.

Trend 2: Video Content and Engagement

Sure, images and text can be interactive to a certain extent, but video content triumphs in enticing your audience. It creates more interaction and audience engagement. Almost all social media platforms like YouTube (obviously), Facebook, Instagram, Snapchat, and even Twitter have witnessed an exemplary engagement with video content, with more shares, likes, and comments. As a marketer, you need to tap into more video content generation compared to images, especially this year. Instead of reading a long paragraph, users are more interested in learning about your product through a video. With around 81 percent of brands using video content to increase engagement, the upcoming years will generate around 82 percent of online traffic from video content.

If your content was made more interactive and engaging, people would be keener on purchasing your products. Until now, marketers believed that videos with shorter spans could engage audiences more, which is completely going to change from now on. Videos of more than five minutes will engage users due to the emotional connection built midway (depending on the type of content, of course). Also, 360-degree videos will be all the rage among marketers. Tap into it before your competitors know about its potential.

Trend 3: Rise of Influencer Marketing

The rise of social media also witnessed a rise in influencers. It is 2020—people are doing what they love and getting paid for it. Many influencers have found their passion and acknowledged their talent using social media platforms. Numerous beauty, fashion, travel, and food bloggers have risen above their insecurities and built their own community on these platforms. With their increase in popularity, brands are making full use of their audience reach. You might have come across numerous brands and influencers collaborating over a product, which majorly benefits both parties. Influencers are getting hefty paychecks for promotions, especially fashion and beauty bloggers. The preferred media for this practice are Instagram and YouTube.

According to a survey conducted by Hootsuite, 48 percent of their clients used celebrities for promotion, and 45 percent used micro-influencers to reach an audience with a smaller radius but tight engagement.

This year, people can expect a major change among all influencers. More and more bloggers are shifting toward promoting their own brands and blogs instead of promoting other businesses. People can also expect a lot of collaborations, with a few big ones starring numerous top-level influencers for mega engagement. As for marketing agencies, they will probably still set budgets to sponsor influencers that are looking for extra content and weighty paychecks. Basically, there is no stopping influencers in 2020—and for many more years to come.

Trend 4: Stories and IGTV Videos

The previous chapter talked about how stories have been a major hit as a new feature for user engagement. Using this impressive add-in to promote your content promises a huge success this year. While Snapchat had the initial concept of disappearing content, Instagram, Facebook, and WhatsApp incorporated this feature into their networks to improve user experience and increase engagement. Instagram is, however, constantly updating this feature, making it useful for marketing agencies and influencers.

With innovative tools like colorful fonts, art features, filters, stickers, and Boomerangs, stories have been extremely popular, and they are here to stay in 2020 as well. You can cross-promote your posts through stories, or link your website with your stories for more followers. Brands are also developing specific story templates to enhance storytelling and increase engagement with their followers.

Since Instagram videos have a limited watching time, the social media platform introduced a new feature called IGTV videos in 2018 that allowed users to watch content from a minute to an hour. Even though IGTV videos went through a rocky start at first, a few tweaks and updates have given them the significance they deserve. They are now extensively used by content marketers and influencers to promote their products and content. IGTV videos seem to have a bright future this year and beyond. Even though the majority of marketers and influencers still opt for YouTube and Facebook to promote video content, IGTV videos should also be considered. Here are some cool ways you can use IGTV videos to promote your content in 2020:

➢ Create portrait or vertically-formatted content that takes up the entire screen, as it enhances usability.

➢ Use a landscape format to reach a bigger audience.

➢ Use the IGTV preview option to get easily discovered in the "Explore" feed.

➢ Create polls and ask questions about the type of video content your followers like to watch. This will increase interaction, and you'll know what your audience loves.

Trend 5: Increase in Shopping

With more and more brands establishing their names daily, people have a myriad of options and products to shop online. And with the powerful tool of social media, every brand is trying to create its own niche to be recognized. Content marketers and advertisers are trying to build brand awareness and identity to entice more customers into buying their products. All this has led to an increase in sales, and social media alone is generating billions of dollars in revenue for brands every year.

The development and marketing of company websites have been in place for a decade, giving birth to e-commerce. However, with the popularity of social media shopping, social e-commerce is now at its peak, showing a promising future for 2020 as well. So, if you are here to understand how to sell your products or services on social media, you're in luck. The numbers speak for themselves. While more than 50 percent of customers discover and find products on Facebook and Instagram, at least 30 percent of them make purchases through social media platforms.

Chief brands like Nike realized this potential, which led them to use the feature of in-app purchases; they have a dedicated Facebook and Instagram shop. This way, your customer can make a purchase while staying within the app, which helps to generate more sales. Instagram has also recently developed a shopping feature that lets you tag up to five products in a post. You can get additional information about the product when you click on the tag. This feature has let brands generate huge amounts of revenue. With additional helpful elements, such as the "swipe up" feature and plug-ins that create invoices and confirmation, social media platforms are further developing their features to enhance social e-commerce.

Trend 6: Incorporation of Augmented Reality for Customers

Even though augmented reality has already been discussed as a major change that can be expected in 2020, it can also be considered a great trend in marketing strategy. Often confused with virtual reality, augmented reality is the incorporation of real-life scenes into computer-based graphics, designed to improve user experience. While Snapchat has already implemented AR filters and used geolocation as a key feature, other social media platforms are also using augmented reality extensively. You must have played Pokemon Go, which was all the rage among users around the globe a few years ago. You could see Pokemons running around in the real world through your camera lens. As much as people enjoyed this feature, they could not help but think more about this pioneering tech.

As you can see, every platform is increasingly making use of this progressive technological innovation. It is time for you to incorporate it into your marketing strategies as well. You can learn from brands like Sephora and Timberland that are using AR as a marketing strategy. Nike is on its way with a few experiments to provide its customers with an interactive experience. The major benefits of using AR for marketing are standing out, fulfilling the expectations of unique content, and selling products at a faster pace than anticipated due to quicker customer decisions.

Even though Snapchat is largely based on AR at present, Facebook and Instagram are also working toward becoming fully AR-based. Until you are introduced to a new innovation, you can start building your marketing plan around the existing augmented reality features that are available and popular across social media platforms, such as filters, bitmojis, maps, and location tags. Again, it can be advantageous to target younger audiences because millennials and Gen Z make up the majority of these users.

While you definitely need to keep an eye on these strategies, it is a good idea to keep exploring and looking for new options and trends that might just boom anytime in today's world. Whether you are using YouTube, Instagram, Twitter, or Facebook, fill in the gaps using strategies that are directed toward individual social media platforms.

Chapter 4: Personal Branding—Are You Doing It Right?

With the market being completely saturated in many fields, most people find it easier to relate to an individual rather than a company. That is why personal branding makes all the difference. However, when it comes to personal branding, you need to understand how to do it right as it can also negatively impact your business's image or reputation.

To help you figure out if you are on the right track or not, you must first understand the difference between personal branding and product branding.

Product Branding

Each brand represents a specific product or service and should portray a certain image to deliver a message through the product or service at hand, as well as taking into consideration the elements of branding such as design, font, color, logo, and overall vibe. Branding is important because it has the power to make the target audience recognize your products instantly and feel a specific way concerning your brand.

Personal Branding

Personal branding, on the other hand, goes a little further. Instead of focusing just on the product or service that your company offers, it focuses on an individual. A personal brand is all about you as a person and the image you choose to portray to the world. Adding a human touch to any brand makes it easier to connect with and more appealing to customers.

Because this type of branding makes it so much simpler for an audience to relate to a person instead of a product or service, using personal branding can have quite successful effects. If you choose to use this method, here are a few tips to make sure you are doing it right:

Clean Out Your Social Media Platforms

If you choose to put yourself out there and use the image that represents your business as a form of personal branding, you need to ensure that your personal social media platforms also align with the brand identity and do not have any negative impact on your brand. While interacting with a face can be extremely effective when it comes to marketing on social media, it can also backfire if you are not careful with the image you put forward. That is why the first thing you need to do is clean up your social media accounts; delete any images or posts that do not correspond with your brand's identity or values, and be wary of what you share on your social media platforms. Choosing to use personal branding means that your actions also reflect that of your brand.

This does not mean that you cannot post anything personal or need to be professional 100 percent of the time; it just means that you need to think twice about the things you post, the tone of voice you use, your language, and how personal you get with your accounts.

Be Consistent

An essential part of using personal branding on social media is consistency. Not only in the images, vibe, and choice of content you post but also in the values that you represent. Say you are trying to promote sustainability. If you are all about saving the environment and raising awareness of the problems of using plastics, you need to ensure that you do not contradict yourself on your social platforms by collaborating with a brand that is harmful to the environment and produces a whole lot of plastic waste. This will not only infuriate your followers but also put your reputation and credibility—as well as your company's reputation—at risk. When it comes to promoting core values, you need to be consistent or separate your business and personal life.

Maintain a Visually Appealing Front

When representing your brand, your profile is no longer your free space to do whatever you want. On the contrary, it should be treated as an extension of your business with a similar brand identity, but with a greater focus on you. That is why you must use high-quality photographs, instead of those just taken on your phone. You should also use the same color palette and harmonious vibes throughout your page. The important thing is that you make your accounts visually appealing as any potential customer or business partner will check out your accounts first before making a deal with you. They need to be greeted with a positive vibe as soon as they access your accounts.

One of the strongest ways to promote a brand is to identify it from a distance. As a tool for personal branding, you also need to adhere to the same values, content, and overall vibe that make your business unique.

Find the Most Suitable Platform for Your Business

There are many different platforms on social media that cater to not only different age groups but different genders or interests. Since the majority of Internet users are on Facebook, you would think that it would be the best tool for social media marketing and creating your own personal branding account to reach a broader audience. However, you could find that the audience on Facebook is not suitable for your brand and not age-appropriate either. While Facebook focuses on content and news, Instagram is a much better platform for a business that is focused mainly on visuals. It is not enough just to follow the guidelines for personal branding; they will only be effective if used on the right medium, where the audience will be able to interact and communicate with the image you are setting.

Analyze Your Audience

Creating a personal brand allows you to keep an eye on your audience through social media and get closer to them. The more you interact with them, the more you will be able to identify what resonates with them the most. This way, you'll get a better understanding of the changes that can be made to ensure your business's success. You'll also be able to gain insight into who else your audience follows and identify key social media influencers that can be beneficial to your brand. This can lead to potential collaborations or ideas regarding what your target audience will be interested in according to their interaction with your posts.

Choose Other Brand Ambassadors

With personal branding, you do not have to expose yourself or become one with your brand in order to have a shot at succeeding. People like to get a feel of the brand through a person, but it doesn't necessarily have to be you. That is why many companies use brand ambassadors to make them the face of the company as a form of personal branding.

However, when choosing a brand ambassador, basing your decision on numbers is not enough. Because they will be the face and image representing your business, you must make your decisions wisely. They need to be not only a good match in terms of aligning with your brand identity and core values but also a public figure that your target audience appreciates and looks up to. They should want to get to know your business more because they represent it. You need to choose someone who will resort to their social media channels and market your products smoothly, without it putting people off.

In most cases, having a brand ambassador can really help you reach a wider audience as they not only have a high following on their social media platforms but are also influential figures in the community with access to your specific target audience. Using brand ambassadors for personal branding opens up different opportunities and exposes your brand to many different channels that can significantly benefit the business. Just be wise in your choices, as any damage that a brand ambassador may cause could end up harming your image, too.

Be Active on Social Media

Representing your business's image through personal branding means that you need to be active to grow a following and keep the existing audience engaged. The frequency of posts may differ according to each platform you are using, but in general, it is essential to keep your audience coming back for more – meaning that you need to be active daily. The more consistent you are, the more your sales will increase, as many people tend to be skeptical at the beginning. However, they will eventually give in as they keep seeing the product being promoted, not only because this makes it constantly remain at the back of their minds, but also because they start to gain more detailed information and get familiar with the product or service with every post they see. If you are wondering how frequently you should be posting, here is the optimum amount of posts per day for each platform based on Buffer's studies and research:

- **Facebook** – it is best to post two times per day. It can be split into once in the morning and another time in the evening to suit different people who access Facebook at various times of the day.

- **LinkedIn** – it is recommended that a business only post once per day because many people on LinkedIn are more interested in finding jobs and are busy at work.

- **Twitter** – it is best to grab your audience's attention by posting five times per day because of the small number of characters allowed per tweet.

- **Pinterest** – it is ideal for a business to post five times a day since many people are very active and continuously flicking through different boards.

- **Instagram** – focus on posting strong visuals one and a half times per day. That means you can post two on one day and one the next to space them out.

Another way of being active on social media and promoting successful personal branding content is by engaging with your community as much as possible. This can be done by organizing a local charity, taking part in a marathon in your local area, or even sponsoring a kids' show. This will help you get familiar with the community as well as promoting your personal branding to show that you are giving back and interested in leaving a positive footprint – instead of just selling your products. It will also appeal to people on a personal level and make them trust your brand even more. Besides, it can open up more opportunities for collaborations and make for useful, appealing content for your social media platforms.

Video Content

Video content is really picking up, and your personal branding needs to incorporate that to keep up with the trend. This can be done through Instagram stories, IGTV on Instagram, or your very own YouTube channel. Just make sure that the content is relevant, catchy, short, appealing to your audience, and in line with your personal image. Providing the audience with what they want to see and what competitors in your industry are doing will help make your personal branding more appealing.

Remember that personal branding is a great way to expand your social media presence and help you connect with a wider audience. It is always easier to trust a business with a face, as it helps you understand the core values of the business and be sure that you are in good hands. However, before you go ahead and expose a certain image to the public, you need to analyze the situation and make sure that the person in question will have a positive impact on your business's reputation, rather than possibly harming it in the future.

Chapter 5: Knowing and Growing Your Audience

Social media can be a very effective tool for marketing, but you need to have a strong social media presence. To do that, you need not only to understand your audience and what appeals to them but also who your target audience is, what makes them unique, and how to appeal to a specific niche to give you an advantage.

Pinpointing Your Audience

One of the most difficult—yet crucial—tasks for any business is to specify a target audience and narrow it down to a niche market that will benefit from your business and find your products or services appealing.

Having a specific target market should already be part of your business plan. However, as you start your business, you will be able to make an even better analysis based on those that are interested in your products or services and interact with your posts. This allows you to narrow down your target audience and market to those who are most likely to buy your products. You'll find that the people in your target audience have common characteristics or interests, such as demographics, behaviors, or hobbies.

You must define your business's target audience as clearly as possible because this will help you benefit from targeted advertising, which allows you to be extremely specific. This way, you spend advertising money only on those most likely to be interested in making a purchase. This not only boosts your sales but also makes the return on investment for every dollar spent on marketing worth it. However, an important question you should ask is, "How do I figure out who my target audience is?" It is not enough just to have an idea of who your products would be suitable for; there are ways to find out who will benefit from your business and are part of the target audience you should be addressing.

Characteristics to Help You Define Your Audience

- Age

You need to understand which generation you are targeting. This will help you adjust your content accordingly, even in your tone of voice, visuals, and especially your ad campaigns. Age is also a factor in deciding what platform is the most suitable and will generate the most profit because different age groups tend to use different social media platforms. It is not essential to pinpoint a specific age, but just an average range to help you make better decisions when it comes to marketing.

- Gender

In some cases, you could find that one gender finds your business more appealing than the other, and knowing this will help you market specific products and posts to them.

- Location

One of the advantages of Facebook is that it is a global network that allows you to target anyone in the world. However, if your products or services only cater to a specific location, it's essential to highlight that. This will allow you to consider several factors, such as geographic areas to target for your promotions or advertising. It will also help you determine the time zone of your audience, allowing you to be present when your customers are most likely to be active so that you can answer their questions and provide excellent customer service through engagement and interaction. It's also imperative for you to accommodate the time zone when scheduling your social media posts as well as ad campaigns.

- **Language**

Your target audience may likely be speaking a different language. Say your business provides Middle Eastern desserts in North America. You could find that your target audience speaks Arabic rather than English, and so, it is important to take into account their dominant language.

- **Budget and Spending Habits**

It is beneficial to gather information about the spending patterns of your target audience. This will help you understand how to price your products and whether your budgeting is effective concerning your audience. Understanding how much they are willing to spend on a product, as well as how frequently they buy items within your price range, will help you get a better idea of how you should approach your pricing and how successful your marketing will be with promotions and sales.

- **Interests**

There are numerous advantages in determining the interests of your target market. You can do this by analyzing the people who regularly interact with your posts and figuring out what they have in common. You could find that most of them like yoga pages, or have a sweet tooth, or even like to travel. These interests, no matter how specific, will really come in handy when it is time to target your social media ads to a specific audience, helping you gain a wider reach of suitable users.

All of the above is extremely useful information that will really help your business, but where do you get that information from? And how do you determine all these factors to help you narrow down who your target audience is? It is simple: analytics. Going on each platform and checking out the available insights will not only help you determine who your target audience is but also gain the necessary insight into which platform to use for which target audience.

Growing Your Audience

Once you are familiar with your target market, the next question you should ask is, "How does my target audience know that my business exists?" Being able to reach and grow your audience is essential for your business to succeed. Luckily, social media can really help you grow your audience, as it allows you to target ads at them specifically once you have gained valuable insight into their characteristics and interests.

Set Fixed Goals

Key factors that will help you grow your audience are a set plan and strategy that will enable you to reach specific users according to their habits. For instance, while Facebook remains the most widely used social media platform, the majority of millennials and younger users are usually found on Instagram, Twitter, or Snapchat, making it more effective to channel your advertising there if that is the age range you are interested in. However, if you're looking to grow a specific platform for business purposes, you could still work on targeting them as they tend to access various platforms.

Having a plan will enable you to create content that will help you reach your goals and work on specific targets. If you are familiar with your target audience and have the specific goal of reaching a broader audience on Facebook, then you can go about creating engaging content, addressing your audience, and filtering your targeting options to ensure that your paid reach is beneficial. This can result in more people interacting with your posts, and liking your page, or buying your products.

When setting goals, one of the most common and effective methods is the S-M-A-R-T method, which stands for the following:

> **Specific**: Make sure that you have clear, defined goals.

> **Measurable**: Set goals that can be measured so that you can analyze your level of success and monitor your achievements.

> **Achievable**: Avoid setting impossible goals and make sure that what you aim for can actually be achieved with the resources you have.

> **Realistic**: Be realistic about the budget, the expected time frame to achieve your goals and the outcome.

> **Time-Sensitive**: Follow a detailed schedule to help you determine how long it would take you to achieve your goals.

Analyze Your Competitors

To stand out, you need to study the market and figure out what your competitors are doing. Once you have analyzed them, you can start identifying the key factors that make their methodology work—what is it that attracts their audience and appeals to them? Answering these questions can help you understand what your business needs to do. You do not necessarily have to copy them, but you do need to understand what their edge is. This way, you will gain more insight into your target audience and work on coming up with a different edge or finding a gap in the market that you can focus on to attract more followers to your business rather than your competitors.

By looking at the content they share, their engagement, and the frequency in which they post, you can create and apply a successful strategy. Choose more relevant content that is more engaging and will appeal better to your target audience. You can analyze your competitors by searching for the probable keywords on each platform.

Create a Brand Voice

There is a certain lingo, tone, and way of speaking that will attract different age groups. So, once you are familiar with your specific target audience, you should start studying how they text, post, and speak, as well as what their interests are to help create a voice for your brand. This will make them feel more encouraged to interact with your posts and build a connection with your business.

You can even use a caption from a trending TV show that this age group watches, or lyrics from a song they listen to when you find it relevant. This will encourage them to engage with your post and therefore help you reach a wider audience.

Enhance Your Reach

There are several factors you need to take into consideration when it comes to reaching a wider audience. From paying for advertisements to posting at the most suitable times that promote the best engagement, you need to make sure that everything you do is verified, studied, and will help you reach that goal.

Here are the best times to post on each platform:

➤ **Facebook**: While 10 a.m. – 3 p.m. on weekdays are usually the safest times to post on Facebook, the most effective time is usually Thursday, between 1 p.m. – 2 p.m.

➤ **Instagram**: Just like Facebook, Thursday is also the best day to post on Instagram, whereas the safest timings for this platform are from Tuesday to Friday between 9 a.m. – 6 p.m.

➤ **Twitter**: The best time to post on Twitter is on Friday, around 9 a.m. – 10 a.m.

➤ **LinkedIn**: Between 3 p.m. – 5 p.m. on Wednesday is the best time to post on this platform.

Scheduling posts for these timings will allow you to capitalize on the most engaging times of each platform and give your posts an extra push to help them reach your target audience, growing it in the process.

Following these proven strategies to identify and grow your target audience will really help boost your sales, strengthen your social media presence, and make your brand look more authentic and appealing to new followers. Once you have figured out who your target audience is and how to appeal to them, the rest is just a piece of cake.

Chapter 6: Which Platform Should You Use?

With the wide range of social media platforms available today, it is understandable to be confused about which one would be the best for your business. After all, there are budget restrictions and tight schedules to adhere to, and you cannot dedicate and distribute equal amounts of your time to every social media platform there is. That would not make any sense, either, because you need to think about your target audience, business type, and goals. Not every platform is meant for you. One of the key factors in successful business marketing is choosing the right platform. And while there are numerous options to choose from, you will now delve into each one to understand what is best for your business this year.

Facebook

Facebook has been thriving for more than a decade now and is undoubtedly one of the best social media platforms to use for marketing a business. It can be beneficial in targeting users between the ages of 25 and 34, with almost an equal balance of gender distribution. Another notable benefit is that most of the users are educated and have a higher income graph, and it can majorly help your business in driving more sales.

When it comes to existing and probable features, Facebook has come a long way in developing tools that are directed toward promotions and business marketing, making it an effective social media platform. It also offers options to post various types of content, such as images, videos, texts, stories, and links, giving you creative flexibility and a blank canvas to promote your business. One of the important factors to consider is Facebook ads. Also known as Marketplace Ads, this feature appears in a sidebar while browsing through the site. You can use this helpful feature by setting budgets and promoting your business to a specific and interested audience. Other useful features for efficient business marketing on Facebook include Facebook contests, sponsored stories, and paid post promotions.

Instagram

Instagram has rapidly climbed the ladder to be ranked as one of the most sought-after social media platforms in 2019. It shows great promise ahead, too. And so, Instagram should definitely be on your list. This platform showcases a great number of users who follow brands and buy from them. Like Facebook, the majority of Instagram's audience also consists of educated people in higher income brackets. This is good news for your business. As for the features, you can use Instagram's business tools that offer direct interaction with your customers and show statistics like user engagement and the number of shares. It allows you to fix your content and promote it the right way to achieve further engagement.

As discussed earlier, Instagram's shopping feature can also come in handy. If your business aims to sell products, Instagram is your best bet, right after Facebook. You can post images, videos, stories, and links within stories to promote your brand and showcase your creativity. If you are thinking of using just two or three social media platforms for marketing, Instagram must be one.

Snapchat

Snapchat has slowly evolved from an entertainment platform into a marketing channel. Many people underestimate the power of Snapchat in marketing their businesses, but it actually has a lot of potentials. The first benefit is the target audience. As previously pointed out, this social media platform mainly attracts younger audiences, especially Gen Z. If your business aims to sell products or services to teenagers and young adults, Snapchat is the answer. Roughly 71 percent of the Gen Z population uses Snapchat regularly. Your content will successfully reach users between the ages of 12 and 34.

Snapchat uses the concept of stories in the form of images and videos. Even though there is a limit to developing content, you are given the flexibility to post constantly, without going overboard. You have a blank canvas each day, and followers often forget the content that you posted previously as it disappears within 24 hours. One major tactic that brands use on Snapchat is creating sponsored filters, as Snapchat users love playing with filters and lenses. Recently, brands like Taco Bell and Gatorade gained massive interaction by creating their own filters. You can also promote your brand by hiring an influencer who will take over your account for a day.

Twitter

Twitter is all about the power of text in a few characters. The majority of the audience on Twitter tends to be between 18 and 29 years of age, making it a viable option to target a younger audience. Again, the bulk of Twitter's audience is educated and falls under higher income brackets. One of the main concepts that Twitter beholds is the use of hashtags to reach a certain audience group or follow the trending topics on the platform.

Twitter offers the options of posting images, videos, and mainly text to voice your opinion or promote your brand. Since around 7,000 tweets are uploaded every second, your content needs to be powerful to be seen and shared across the platform. Twitter is actually a great way to interact with your audience, and it demands content that drives more engagement. Remember the humorous feud between Taco Bell and Old Spice; it created amazing engagement and promoted the brands.

There is great potential for advertisements on Twitter, too. You can either choose from Twitter's ad format options or promote your brand's tweet to encourage engagement. Another feature that is provided by this platform is Twitter chats, which can be used for maximum interaction and gaining followers.

YouTube

While YouTube is restricted to video content marketing, it can still be used effectively. The scope of video content was mentioned earlier, and YouTube stands true to being a great marketing platform. With around 74 percent of users watching brand-produced content, 90 percent of which watch videos on a smartphone or laptop, YouTube offers great potential to reach a massive audience. It is one of the biggest platforms that have a major influencer impact. Numbers show that more than 50 percent of users have reacted positively to the content and responded well to the products displayed.

With no limit to uploading content, you can stretch your video's content according to the engagement it receives. You can also link or share your video to other social media platforms, increasing the quality of your content presentation. Use call-to-action tools to increase engagement, such as linking your Facebook or Instagram accounts, requesting subscriptions, likes, and shares, and providing a direct path to your blog or website. YouTube also provides you with a big SEO benefit, as Google can directly display a path to your YouTube video if the keywords match.

TikTok

TikTok is a great platform for content creators who are just starting out and want instant recognition. You will find the majority of the Gen Z audience on this recently viral social media platform. Following the same concept of stories and IGTV videos that last from nine to 15 seconds, TikTok has attracted around 500 million users around the world. It is still debatable whether or not it's the right platform for marketing your business, however.

If you are planning to keep your brand identity subtle and composed, TikTok is not for you. It is rather rushed and wacky. If you want some humor and creativity to be continuously incorporated into your content, this platform can help you with it. You can either show the features of your products or create a few short "how-to" videos instead of creating memes that could backfire on your marketing strategy. For instance, the cosmetic brand Lush regularly uploads videos showing the making of their products, which garners attention. You can also collaborate with TikTok influencers who have a massive impact on their audiences. Before taking action, you should discover the platform more and make an informed decision.

LinkedIn

Leaning more toward the professional side, LinkedIn can connect you with potential partners or customers. If you plan to start a business that requires professional connections, and you are willing to hire employees, LinkedIn is the right platform for you. You can constantly post findings, studies, demographics, or milestones achieved by your company, which will be seen on the main feeds of your connections. With 32 percent of users having acquired a degree and 24 percent holding certifications, the bulk of your audience on LinkedIn will fall under average or higher income brackets.

It is a great platform to generate B2B leads and create ads that promote brand awareness. You can also send personalized messages to your followers or audience when they are active to boost interaction. LinkedIn also has influencers and executives that can create a huge impact on the targeted audience. Even if your brand or business does not possess a corporate identity, you can still use LinkedIn as a plausible tool for gaining your audience's attention.

Pinterest

If the majority of your marketing strategy is based on image branding, Pinterest is the right platform for you. This social media platform acts as a brochure of images that target all disciplines, from art to fitness, and from home decoration to fashion advice. It attracts audiences based on aesthetics. A large part of Pinterest's audience is women (around 79.5 percent), who tend to browse the platform for various purposes. A chief factor that can be converted into an advantage is that you can find people from all age groups on Pinterest, mainly between the ages of 18 and 65, most of whom are educated. If you own a women-centric brand, especially if it targets mothers or women who are expecting, you must tap into Pinterest. Almost eight out of ten moms use Pinterest in the United States, which can be a significant benefit.

You can use a Pinterest business account, connect your other social media accounts to it, claim your website, put in contact details for customers to get in touch with you and create your board. Pinterest also allows for advertising and inserting links to your pins. Use the analytics tool to learn more about popular pins and to get more interaction. Produce your content in a vertical frame range to suit the Pinterest layout and to make it more aesthetically pleasing.

These social media platforms can be—and commonly are—used for effective business marketing. Now, that does not mean you should use them all. As a marketer, you definitely need to tap into Facebook, Instagram, Snapchat, YouTube, and Twitter, among other platforms, as these show a lot of promise this year and beyond. Depending on the type of business and content, you need to measure the potential that each platform will offer. If you do not feel the need, don't waste your time signing up for all these platforms, as that will take a toll on your budget and the quality of your content. Instead, focus on just two or three platforms if you are just starting out, and gradually build on that once you have established a dedicated audience.

Chapter 7: Facebook Marketing

Facebook remains the most widely used social media platform and therefore is essential for most businesses regarding marketing on social media. According to Pew Internet's statistics, roughly two-thirds of American adults use Facebook regularly. That accounts for almost 68 percent, making it an excellent medium to use for adults, as most people are already frequent users.

However, for marketing on Facebook to be effective, there are many factors you need to understand and take into consideration to ensure that you are doing it right. That is why you must know what strategies to follow to improve your Facebook marketing and get the most out of a medium that is widely spread and actually quite cheap to advertise on. To do that, here are a few strategies:

Strategy 1: Engaging Content

One of the first things you need to understand is Facebook's algorithm. The idea behind it—and the reason why it is extremely beneficial—is based on hiding boring content. Because the platform is designed to keep people on it for as long as possible, Facebook has a way of only making interesting or successful content visible to its users. The question is: "How does Facebook make this decision, or label something as boring content?" It's pretty simple. Facebook analyzes the content and classifies it according to the engagement on the post. This means that if the post has likes, comments, or shares, it will be considered interesting, and Facebook will allow it to be seen by many users. However, if a post does not generate any engagement, then Facebook will automatically hide it from users and classify it under boring content. What does this tell us? For your business's posts to be seen, you need to create engaging content for your users.

One of the key aspects that makes Facebook unique and adds an advantage to any business is that Facebook does not just hide boring content, but does the exact opposite if it determines your content is attention-grabbing. That means, if your posts are getting organic interaction, Facebook will give them an extra push by making them visible to more people. That is why any business needs to try and capitalize on that feature by creating the sort of content that will not only appeal to their target audience but will also start a conversation and make them feel the need to comment or share on their own feed.

You would be surprised to know that comments make a huge difference when it comes to recognizing engagement and affecting your post's visibility. The longer the comment, the better, and the more visible your post will be to other users. So, how can you use this information and apply it to your business?

Create Content That Generates an Emotional Response

With the number of photos uploaded on Facebook reaching a staggering 350 million each day, you need to ensure what you are offering is not just like everybody else. That is why the best way of making the users notice your posts is by introducing content that generates emotion. Whether it makes them laugh or cry, fills their heart with warmth, or even provokes them, you need to be able to push a button to get them to interact with your post. Sometimes, it's enough just to make them smile, and you will find them tagging their friends and liking or sharing the post, giving it the opportunity to be more widely spread. So, when you decide to boost it, Facebook will help it reach a wider audience, making your marketing effective at an even lower cost per viewer.

Before you post any content on Facebook or think of what you'll be sharing next on your business's page, ask yourself what kind of emotion it generates. If it looks like it won't trigger an emotion, then find something that will instead.

Use Trending Content to Your Advantage

Being timely not only makes your content relatable but also encourages people to interact and engage with your post as it is something that is happening in the now. Because most people are on Facebook regularly, they tend to get their information from there. So, when a business manages to capitalize on a trend, it instantly gains the attention of the users. Take, for example, the fires in Australia that destroyed thousands of acres of land and a large amount of wildlife. As it was happening, photos of injured koalas and kangaroos were being shared excessively, as this kind of content contains both factors, generating an emotional response, and being timely.

As a business, you could use this to your advantage by either sending a percentage of your proceeds to help those in need in Australia or just writing an emotional post showing the human side of your business. Capitalizing on trending content is a great tool that offers instant rewards and results when it comes to Facebook marketing.

Strategy 2: Video Content

While the rise in video content has already been visible throughout the past couple of years, in 2020, it is expected to increase even more. That is why it's time to resort to videos if you haven't started already. However, there is a specific strategy you need to follow in order to reach your audience and ensure success. Why are videos more effective when it comes to Facebook marketing? Because they get WAY more engagement than photos and text put together! The difference in numbers is not only astounding but also makes it absolutely vital for a business to make use of the effect of videos.

However, most businesses tend to make the mistake of producing promotional or advertorial video content without first building a relationship with their customers. This can make them uninterested in viewing the promotional video you have uploaded, as they are probably unprepared for it. So, how do you get them interested? There is a proven strategy to help develop a relationship and build rapport with your audience first, in order to make video content effective. This is done by using the 3x3 video strategy of "why", "how", and "what" videos. In this technique, you first build a portfolio of videos that help introduce you as a person and your business idea, along with videos explaining what your process looks like. This can be created in the form of "how-to" videos that will appeal to your audience before introducing the "why" videos, which will be presenting why your products are unique or would benefit the user.

"Why" Videos

As a marketer, you can use the "why" videos to really help your audience connect with your business on a personal level. It is a form of personal branding that allows the user to identify the face behind the business and get to know the backstory. Through this process, you will summarize your story and explain the reason you created your business. It is a simple "why" serving to put your idea across and familiarize people with you and your business. It's essential to start with this step to build successful video content. Think of questions like the following:

➢ What motivated you to start?

➢ What are you known for?

➢ What are you most proud of?

➢ What problems did you face?

➢ What was missing in the market?

In this category, you should start out with three different videos of about 20 to 90 seconds, explaining who you are and the story behind your business. When producing the videos, you should try and focus on reaching a different target audience each time, as you might later notice that one video was more appealing to men, while another was more appealing to women.

"How" Videos

For your next set of three videos, you should present a series of "how" or "how-to" videos. In these, you get the chance to explain the entire process your business goes through to come up with the final product—your audience will hopefully appreciate the work and effort that goes into it. "How to" videos are popular to such an extent that 51 percent of the traffic on YouTube comes from them. While it is a different platform with a slightly different audience, it goes to show just how important it is for your business to produce "how-to" videos.

In this category, you should produce three different videos, each with a different story. Your first video in the "how" series can emphasize explaining how your products come to life, from an initial idea to a final product. It will help your audience have a deeper understanding of how unique your products are, while also getting to know you and your business.

You can further use "how-to" videos to provide your customers with tips and give them some information they can use to create simpler versions of your products at home or even something that can go with your products. For example, if your business is selling ceramic bowls or dishes, your "how-to" series can focus on tips to take into consideration while cleaning the plates or heating them, or even possibly an easy recipe using the plates. You can get creative and see what resonates the most with your audience.

"What" Videos

In this section, you will already have created a relationship with your customers that allows you to start promoting your products. Now is the time to post videos to help you promote the products' unique selling points. In these videos, you can make the audience feel the need to purchase your products.

The "why", "how", and "what" videos are great to get you started on your video content journey on Facebook. However, there are some other aspects you need to consider while you are putting this method into practice.

Additional Tips

- **Only Spend Money on Effective Videos**

Many businesses make the mistake of spending money trying to boost videos that do not appeal to the audience. However, when it comes to video content, the average amount you should be spending is $8-10 for every 1,000 views. If you invest $8 and you only get 500 views or less, then this should be an indication that you need to stop spending more money on your video. That money will be going to waste due to a problem in the content itself, and Facebook is classifying it as "boring".

- **Facebook Video Content Strategy is a Long-Term Plan**

This process could take from six to 12 months. With video content, understanding your audience will take time, so it is important to have patience. During this time, you should know that one out of ten videos will work, meaning that 90 percent of your videos will not. If you need to have ten successful videos, you need to create 100 videos until you get them right.

- **The Ideal Duration is Between 20 and 90 Seconds**

The sweet spot usually hits at the 60th second. Take that into consideration when producing your video content, and try not to make it too long or too short.

- **Monitor Your ThruPlay**

ThruPlay can help you analyze how effective your videos are. It is an optimization and billing tool option for video ads that help you understand whether your video is worth boosting or not. ThruPlay yields the ideal results when it's played until the end or at least for 15 seconds.

- **Test Your Videos on Different Audiences**

Analyze your videos after a week to understand who should be your target audience and cater to them accordingly.

Strategy 3: Facebook Ads

71 billion dollars is spent on TV ads that nobody watches. While the viewership of television has already gone down immensely, those who do still watch tend to hit the mute button when it is time for commercials or to get a snack, go to the bathroom, or do anything else except actually watch the commercial on the screen. So, why do businesses still resort to paying large sums of money to use an advertising technique that is no longer effective? Ask yourself a simple question to understand just how useless ads have become: "How many times have I clicked on the 'Skip Ad' option that appears on the screen when watching a video?" Most people have never watched a single ad, making it a huge waste of money.

On the other hand, Facebook ads are not only extremely cheap in comparison to the market, but are also very effective to reach a wider audience and grow a business's presence online. However, with Facebook's algorithm constantly changing, you can find yourself spending large sums of money on content that is not effective. To help you have a better understanding of the best way to use Facebook ads to your advantage, here are some key factors you should understand:

Types of Facebook Ads

As a marketer or business owner, the first thing you should understand is what type of ads you could use.

- **Image Ads**

This type of advertisement is one of the simplest and easiest ways to start advertising on Facebook. This is done by choosing to promote one of the images that you have already shared to your Facebook page by boosting an existing post.

- **Video Ads**

Because video is a key marketing tool, video advertising is another way you can choose to use Facebook marketing to your advantage. Your boosted videos can appear on your audience's feeds or on Facebook stories when they have a shorter duration. You can even consider using GIFs or animation in your video content instead of live videos.

- **Video Poll Ads**

While it is only available on mobile devices, this type of Facebook ad requires the audience to become more interactive, making it a tool to increase brand awareness.

- **Carousel Ads**

With carousel ads, your business can highlight different products or services, or even use them to shed light on unique benefits or advantages of a specific product. This is because carousel ads allow you to use up to ten images or videos together.

- **Slideshow Ads**

A slideshow ad puts together a series of still photos, text, or videos from your feed and creates a short video ad. It is a useful tool to showcase a variety of products or services your business offers.

- **Collection Ads**

Another tool designed specifically for mobile devices, this option allows you to put together up to five products that customers can click on to buy, making it an extremely effective tool as it is a direct selling opportunity on Facebook.

- **Lead Ads**

Also designed for mobile devices, this tool allows you to gather information quickly from the users without much typing. This can be used to collect contact info for a newsletter or product trial, in addition to easily receiving questions or feedback.

- **Dynamic Ads**

Dynamic ads are used to help you target users who are already interested in your products but have not made a purchase yet. This type of ad appears on their Facebook feeds, featuring a specific product they have previously searched about or added to their carts. This gives them an extra nudge to make the purchase.

- **Messenger Ads**

With the huge number of people using Facebook Messenger as a texting app, Messenger ads give you access to 1.3 billion people every month. All you have to do is choose Messenger as the desired placement for your ad, and it will only be visible to people using Messenger.

- **Story Ads**

The launch of Facebook stories created another avenue to promote an ad or small video and reach your audience faster. When users access stories, they are already in the right mood to watch whatever comes their way, making it a good time to market your products.

How to Advertise on Facebook

If you already have a Facebook page for your business, then you can follow these steps to create successful ads using Facebook Ads Manager:

- **Step 1: Choose the Objective of Your Advertisement**

One of the great things about Facebook ads is that they offer a variety of marketing objectives for you to choose from to help you optimize your ads and get the best results. To select one that is appropriate for your business needs, you can log into Facebook Ads Manager, click on the Campaigns tab, then select Create to start a new campaign. You will find 11 different marketing objectives, such as brand awareness, reach, traffic, and many others to choose from based on the objective you need for your business.

- **Step 2: Find a Suitable Title for Your Campaign**

The next step is to name your ad campaign to monitor it on the Facebook Ads Manager. In this step, you will also be able to choose the focus of the posts and decide whether you want to highlight post engagement, page likes, or event responses.

- **Step 3: Enter Ad Account Details**

To get your ads up and running, you need to set up your ad account by entering key information. Click on Set Up Ad Account and fill in the necessary details such as country, currency, and time zone.

- **Step 4: Target the Right Audience**

One of the advantages of Facebook as a marketing platform is that it allows you to focus on specific criteria in targeting your audience, unlike any other platform. To start choosing the target audience for your ads, open your Facebook ad campaign, and choose which page to promote. Then, scroll down until you find the option that allows you to add a custom audience of people who are already familiar with your business.

The next step is to choose your target location, age, gender, and language. As you add more optimizations, the approximate reach indicator displayed on the right side of the screen will work more accurately.

To increase the return on investment, you need to use detailed targeting to reach the correct target audience.

➢ Detailed Targeting: In this field, you'll be able to decide whom to target based on demographics, interests, and behaviors. This is where you can get really specific and choose to target people who follow bridal stores, for example.

➢ Connections: You can either choose to target your audience or someone who has interacted with your page before, or choose to exclude them entirely to reach new audiences by selecting Exclude people who like your page. However, if your main focus will be your existing audience, then you can select People who like your page.

- **Step 5: Choose Where Your Ad Will Appear**

The next step is to decide where your ads will show. There is an option that allows your ads to appear on Facebook, Instagram, and Messenger, allowing you to get through to a different audience on several platforms by using the Automatic Placements option.

However, you could also choose to specify a type of device, platform, or placement, such as feeds, stories, messages, or even articles.

- **Step 6: Budgeting**

Once you have a fixed budget set, it is time to decide how to allocate that money to the Facebook ad campaign. You can select a daily or lifetime budget and decide on the start and end dates. Then, you decide whether you want the ad to go live straight away or schedule it for a time in the future. Keep in mind that you can choose an optional cost and bid control to ensure you do not go over budget, as there is a cap in place per action rather than for the overall campaign.

- **Step 7: Create Your Ad**

After choosing your ad format based on your objectives, you can use the preview tool at the bottom of the page to get an idea of how your ad will appear in different placements. Once you are satisfied, you can click the green Confirm button to submit the order and then wait for an email confirmation from Facebook to notify you of the ad approval.

Facebook ads are becoming a cheap alternative to many other types of advertising, and they are much more effective. That is why your business must understand how to make the most of Facebook advertising and capitalize on it while it's still relatively cheap. With these tools and tips, you will have a basic understanding of how your business can benefit from Facebook marketing.

Chapter 8: YouTube Marketing

Now that you have learned about Facebook marketing, it is time to delve into another popular social media platform. After hearing enough praise about YouTube being an effective marketing platform, you have to include it in your plan if you haven't yet. This chapter talks about how you can use YouTube to extensively promote your brand, mentioning three optimum strategies and additional tips to execute to achieve success.

Apart from being one of the top social media platforms, YouTube is also the second-largest search engine, following Google. It was mentioned earlier how video marketing is more effective compared to image and text marketing. With YouTube generating 300 to 400 hours of videos every hour, and with a billion daily users, there is no reason for you not to use this platform.

However, building your community and brand awareness can be difficult due to millions of channels that are collectively thriving on this platform. There is so much competition that building your niche and getting recognized could be a major task. To help you overcome these challenges and promote effective brand awareness and engagement, here are a few strategies to use in YouTube marketing this year.

Strategy 1: Optimized Content

Content is king. It is what will attract a broader audience and create more engagement on your channel, helping you grow your brand. Optimizing and tweaking your content to gain more interaction and followers is the number one strategy toward effective marketing. Here is how you can optimize your content for this purpose.

Make a Content Plan

To create an effective content plan, you need to know and follow these three guiding principles:

- **Discover Your Audience**

Even though this has been extensively talked about, this point is restricted solely to YouTube marketing. Once you know your brand, you will know the age group and gender of your target audience. Do some research into the type of videos that they currently watch and their behavior on this platform.

- **Know and Study Your Competition**

You know what they say: "Keep your friends close and your enemies closer." Well, you don't exactly have enemies here because it is all about healthy competition. Knowing about brands and companies within your discipline and the marketing strategies they use can be beneficial. You can watch their videos and point out mistakes or problems that you can avoid in order to improve your content.

- **Set Goals**

Why are you doing this? What is your main objective? Is it to sell more products? Is it to drive more engagement? Ask yourself questions, and set your ultimate goals accordingly. It will give you a clear idea of the right direction toward producing optimum content.

Type of Content

Now that you have created an effective content plan, it is time to explore the types of content that you could use for your brand's marketing. It will, of course, majorly depend on whether you want to sell your products or simply generate more views and interaction. It'll also depend on your target audience and what they prefer to watch, as pointed out earlier. Whether you are managing a fashion brand or opening a food and beverage company, you need to understand your brand and the type of content that'll attract more people to it. Any content created without a purpose or concrete intent is bound to fail.

There are many types of content that bloggers—or in this case, vloggers—use to gain more followers. If you are confused about where to start, you can choose from the existing types that are highly preferred by viewers, such as product reviews, unboxing videos, DIY projects, educational videos, comedy, and "how-to" videos, among several others. These are extremely popular and successful in garnering attention. Or you can experiment with a certain type of content and come up with your own style. It will help your brand stand out and be easily recognized.

Practice Consistency

It is really important to upload content consistently, and this applies to all social media platforms. Now, by consistency, this does not just mean uploading videos regularly; it is rather about uploading a certain type of content that follows a pattern. You must have heard about being consistent multiple times, but what most people don't tell you is how to do it, which is exactly what this book is about. But before the "how", you need to know "why". The answer is that consistency keeps your followers excited and gives them a purpose. It raises expectations that are fulfilled by your videos constantly. Also, YouTube is designed with an algorithm that spreads your content to a bigger audience if you post consistently.

As for the "how", you can start by maintaining an upload schedule—a realistic one. You cannot simply set the goal of uploading a video every two days when you need at least three to four days to shoot and edit it. Prepare a plausible schedule and stick to it. You can set templates for your videos and fix certain factors, such as the fonts and editing type, to keep things flowing. Depending on your content, you can also shoot a long video beforehand and split it into three or four parts to have content for the following days.

Use SEO for Video Titles and Descriptions

It has been mentioned how search engine optimization can affect the discovery of your videos. Because YouTube is a search engine, you can use SEO on this platform to rank your videos higher than others within the same niche. SEO is basically when you insert certain keywords, mostly words or phrases, into your video titles and descriptions based on the common words searched by users. Make sure that they are relevant to your content. You can also add them to your closed captions or subtitles. However, you cannot use all the keywords within your title; it will just make it sound nonsensical. This is where tags come in handy; you can put around ten to 20 tags below every video, which is where you can add those keywords for further search optimization.

And when it comes to captions, since YouTube automatically generates most of the captions, there are high chances of them being inaccurate. You can fix this by adding your own closed captions. This will allow you to add your preferred keywords and present the right information to your audience. You should also consider translating your video into other languages to engage audiences worldwide. This way, YouTube will rank your video higher due to keywords in other languages.

Strategy 2: YouTube Stories

Following in the footsteps of Snapchat, Instagram, Facebook, and WhatsApp, YouTube has also introduced the feature of stories for channels that have 10,000 or more subscribers. YouTube Stories was launched in 2018, and since then, it has offered an additional benefit to the channels and influencers to stay further updated with their subscribers. It looks promising this year, as well.

Stories are commonly viewed as a major engagement tool now, with one-third of the total viewers watching stories and content produced by small and big brands. Companies are actively using the concept of stories and making it an integral part of their advertising plan. The key is to stand out. It all comes down to how well you use this feature, and whether you get the maximum benefit out of it.

Now that the overall importance of stories is clearer, it is time to delve into a few aspects of YouTube Stories to understand it better.

Benefits of using YouTube Stories

Even though it is not an original concept, YouTube Stories offers its own set of benefits due to a few differences and extra features. Here are four amazing ways you can benefit from using YouTube Stories for your content marketing:

- **They Remain on The Feed for Seven Days**

Earlier known as YouTube Reels, these stories stay on your feed for a week, unlike Snapchat, Instagram, and Facebook stories that disappear within 24 hours. It is a major benefit as you can create a compelling storytelling background that lasts for days, and it can be viewed by your potential subscribers days after your upload. Your followers can also view it the next day in case they missed some important content. You can mold your content according to the number of days available. It also keeps your audience aware of your content.

- **They Reach Potential Subscribers**

These also target and engage users who have not subscribed to your channel yet, allowing you to increase your followers. It is a great peek-a-boo strategy to use in triggering curiosity among your present and future subscribers. Even if you are not a subscriber, you can view the stories of other channels and influencers that are trending right on your home page.

• They Open Up New Opportunities

Stories are a bonus to every content marketer these days, especially this year. They make for light-weight content, are easy to create, and have a heavy impact on interaction with users. Since YouTube's main concept is based on video content, stories are specifically useful for this platform. YouTube also gives you the flexibility to unleash your creativity with its tools, such as font types, filters, stickers, music, and much more.

• They Are Simple and Practical

Stories can be images or video-formatted content that can either contain plain text or simple pictures of your products. You can also use a few snippets from your video, without putting any extra effort to shoot content for your stories.

Through YouTube Stories, you, as a marketer or content creator, will have the opportunity to create extremely light content as opposed to the heavy shots and edited videos that you usually upload. Other great ideas for stories can be behind-the-scenes footage, random and fun interviews with your team members, handing over your stories to an influencer, product reviews, or "how-to" video content like tutorials, discount announcements or giveaways, or a sneak peek of your upcoming campaigns. This is the perfect way to create humorous, entertaining, and engaging content.

Impact on Users

Users are much more open to viewing stories than long heavy videos of more than four to five minutes. Since the average attention span of the majority of users is usually short, stories are the perfect way to capture their attention. So much so that around 63 percent of Instagram and Snapchat users view stories. Around 70 percent of those are American, the majority of which falls under the millennial and Gen Z generations.

YouTube Stories have been perceived more as entertaining content rather than informative guides. They have had an emotional effect on users, grabbing their complete attention—most users stated that they were entirely invested and were "looking for more." Your stories do not need to be perfect, heavily edited, or "staged"; they are ideal for creating a more authentic image of your brand and showing your audience the real scenario.

Creating Stories and Garnering Responses

YouTube Stories can be viewed on the front page of the app, with the highlight being the user's profile picture. You just need to click the Create button, followed by Story. Press the capture button to take pictures or hold it to shoot videos. Edit your content using a wide range of available text options, stickers, and music. You can also directly upload a picture or a video from your phone gallery.

Users can also react and comment on your stories and others' comments with a thumbs up, thumbs down, or a heart icon. You can reply to your followers' comments with images or videos, making it more interactive. However, it would have been more successful if you were provided with a "swipe up" option to link your website to your stories like on Instagram.

What Does its Future Look Like?

While Snapchat and Instagram have been successful in introducing the stories feature, YouTube still has some catching up to do regarding other social media platforms. A few users and critics lashed out at YouTube for adding in the already-overused concept of stories. A few channels and influencers were also upset about the limitation of getting to use the feature only after gathering a community of 10,000 subscribers, which can prove to be difficult on a highly competitive platform like YouTube.

While smaller channels and brands would have to struggle their way toward growth, the already-established channels will gather more followers by using the stories feature. However, if YouTube works on a few issues like opening the option of stories to smaller brands, replying to comments with text, and linking websites with the "swipe up" feature, among others, it is bound to succeed in the coming years.

Strategy 3: YouTube Advertising

YouTube ads are undeniably the best way to promote and sell your products, mainly due to the power of video content. Even if you have developed a stellar video campaign, it is worthless if it does not reach a massive audience. This is where YouTube ads can help. You might have come across ads related to specific products or services that you've recently searched for. When the video content relates to the product you desire, you are bound to watch the entire video for more knowledge. This is how YouTube ads work; by targeting specific keywords and searches.

Types of YouTube Ads

There are three types of YouTube ads to choose for your business:
- **TrueView Ads**

The skippable ads that you see at the beginning of any video are known as TrueView ads. While they are flexible and allow you to experiment with your type of content, they also allow the viewers to use the call-to-action button, increasing the interaction. A major benefit of TrueView ads is that you do not pay for the ad unless your viewer has watched more than 30 seconds of it, or used the call-to-action button. This saves you money on viewers who aren't genuinely interested.

- **Pre-Roll or Non-Skippable Ads**

Running anywhere between 15 and 20 seconds, pre-roll ads are non-skippable ads that appear before the main video starts playing, or in the middle of long videos (also known as mid-roll ads). They were extremely annoying when they were first introduced, but viewers have now gotten used to them. Your company can benefit from these as you have the maximum potential to create a commercialized and focused ad for the interested viewers who will watch the entire video ad. Following a pay-per-click concept for payment, this method offers a suitable space for your ad. This type of ad also includes a call-to-action button for the interested viewers.

- **Bumper Ads**

Typically lasting for six seconds, bumper ads are optimized for mobile phones and are the shortest option for delivering important content. These are non-skippable as well, but much more tolerable due to their shorter duration. Acting as "highlights" or reminders of important products, events, or launches, bumper ads are seen at the end of the main videos. Similar to YouTube Stories, you can either show glimpses of the next launch, sneak peeks of your new products, or a piece of exciting news related to your business.

As powerful as YouTube marketing may be, do not forget to promote your content across various social media platforms. That is the only way to be seen and recognized among millions of other brands. Hire YouTube influencers that have a large fan base to present your business creatively, or opt for cross-promotion. YouTube is a great way to promote your business, and you should start posting the right content and being consistent on your channel as soon as possible.

Chapter 9: Twitter Marketing

A few years ago, using Twitter as a marketing platform was off the charts. However, as time passed, content creators and marketers realized the importance of Twitter, which allowed them to interact directly with their customers, use images and visuals to create authenticity, and present their brand as human. Basically, Twitter allowed all brands and companies to present their raw image to the world, helping in building emotional connections and driving more attention to them. So, it grew as an important marketing platform over the years.

Twitter has, in fact, boomed so much that a few brands use this platform as their primary tool for marketing. And it is suggested that you include it in your main marketing platforms as well. Do not worry if you are just starting out; this chapter details some tips and strategies to help you sail your Twitter boat and be recognized easily within the saturated market.

First, to prepare the strategies that you will be defining for successful campaigns, a few of these tips can help you effectively plan and follow the framed strategies. Even though some of these were discussed earlier, some are necessary to be revised for a favorable outcome in the context of Twitter marketing.

Setting Targets and an Ultimate Goal

To frame a set of targets, you need to ask yourself a few questions: "What's the main objective of launching my brand on Twitter? Do I want to generate revenue by sales? Or do I simply want to create a brand image?" You can also use this platform to increase your customers' loyalty and improve your customer service. You need to list all the reasons and objectives that you are expecting from all campaigns, which will help you in generating content accordingly. It will help you form a clear marketing plan and aim directly at your main goal.

So, once you have defined your targets and started following a solid plan, you can track your progress and keep an eye on your team's performance. Your company will be setting a budget for social media marketing, and it is your job to create a realistic plan and set the strategies that will produce the targeted return on investment.

Number of Accounts

Whether your company consists of a bunch of people just starting out or it is a multifaceted company that has many departments, you need to think about the number of accounts that will be up and running. If you already have a Twitter account with a certain number of followers, that shows great potential—it's recommended that you turn it into a business account for your company. Consider the departments or separate teams within your company and think about whether having separate accounts would be more effective or not.

Planning Your Content

To plan your content and build a specific style, you need to know what your target audience wants. You know how important it is by now because it has been emphasized throughout the book. It paves a clear path for the type of content you want to create, and the pattern that will attract your followers. It is also important to analyze your competition and know the type of content they are posting. You surely want to stand out and create your own identity within the market.

Four Great Ways of Planning

● *Live Video Tweets*

You know the importance of video content marketing and how users are more attracted to this kind of content. A few years ago, Twitter, like other social media platforms, introduced the live video feature, which has been quite successful. You can use this to show behind-the-scenes footage of your business and increase interaction with your followers. Around 80 percent of users tend to remember the videos they watch online. This is a real-time strategy that works wonders for marketing your brand. Your followers have the opportunity to catch a glimpse of the faces behind your brand, and this curiosity drives further engagement.

● *Threaded Tweets*

At times, your marketing plan will be saturated with short tweets and videos. This is when threaded tweets can make a difference. Connecting threads to your tweets increase curiosity among your followers and lets you tell a story instead of limiting it to a few characters. It is now easy for you to share a product review, inform your followers about a launch or event in detail, or simply create an irresistible storytelling tactic. This feature allows you to add more text to further threads once the original tweet is published.

● *Highlighting Social Causes*

If your brand supports a particular social cause, it is necessary to keep it highlighted within your content all the time. From wars to climate change, there is always an ongoing concern or issue around the world. As a global channel, you need to show your concern and take a stand against such issues—your followers will expect nothing less. Once you have established a massive channel, you have the power of reaching millions of people simultaneously and creating major awareness. This will not only help in connecting your brand with like-minded people but also in making your channel stand out by creating a lot of engagement. The "Tweet for a Cause" hashtag has been popular on the platform, and rightly so.

Whenever a major social, cultural, or political issue arises, the "Twitterati" are the ones who respond the fastest. People see many debates and concerns being voiced by people of various nationalities and backgrounds through their tweets. You should consider this neglected factor and use it to your advantage.

● *Marking Important Events or Days*

People around the world celebrate special occasions, festivals, and events that are either globally dominant or are specific to a particular country or community. Marking these events on your calendar and producing content accordingly can help in creating more audience engagement. For instance, India celebrates Diwali, which is an important festival for the country. Creating content that revolves around Diwali and your brand image can garner a lot of attention from India, helping you gain plenty of followers—and probably an increase in sales—due to its massive population.

Another example of an event that reflected on Twitter was the Golden Globes in 2018. The hashtag "2018#GoldenGlobes" went viral, which was followed by numerous relevant tweets. You just need to keep an eye on the calendar and look for events within your region and around the world. It can be anything related to music, festivals, sports, fashion, movies, etc. Try to attend as many events as you can, especially if they are relevant to your brand. Live-tweet while you are there, or take as many photos as you can. Just pay attention to the happenings around you to stay updated.

These methods of creating engagement can surely be helpful, but three specific strategies can help your brand have an edge and lead to massive interaction with your audience—and which are often ignored by other accounts:

Strategy 1: Personalized Responses

Providing your followers with personal responses, no matter which channel they are using, is a great way of gaining their trust and increasing overall interaction. It proves that there are human operators behind your brand, which can play a major role in building an approachable brand image.

Using Sarcasm and Humor

Again, people know how sarcasm and humor can win over a massive number of users. You can use it to show a lighter side of your brand. There are many funny GIFs available online that can be used to prove your point without offending customers and followers. Being consistent in portraying clever humor keeps your followers waiting for more content and responses from your end.

A few examples of brands that consistently use wit within their content and responses are Netflix, KFC, Oreo, and Moosejaw. These brands know how to keep their content original and fresh, as well as keep their fans entertained with clever responses. You can take a more in-depth look at these brands and their marketing strategies to learn more.

However, the stats show that 88 percent of followers dislike sarcastic responses to their inquiries, and feel like brands are mocking them. This could lead to the downfall of you and your brand name, so it is better to avoid using humor if you do not have an aptitude for it. Even if your post goes viral, it could lead to many negative responses instead of positive ones. In this case, it's wiser to avoid the banter and take a more straightforward path.

Social Listening

When buying a product, people place their trust in you and want to receive their money's value. If they are not satisfied with your products or services, it is their right to complain and ask for refunds. You need to listen to your customers' queries and complaints and address them to build an authentic and trustworthy brand. However, stay away from customers who are simply taking advantage of potentially free products or illegitimate refunds.

Try to respond to customers personally by replying to their tweets or sending a private message. Leave your email address or contact details to take it further from there.

Twitter Chats

Using Twitter chats is the ultimate way to grow more connections and followers by delving into the right kind of chat topics with like-minded people and brands. It demands you to be active with conversations, following people and keeping the relations alive after exiting the chat. This is a great way to attract not only random followers but also those who will value your brand and promote it sincerely. You can also start your own chat if you have difficulty in finding one that will help you "fit in". Either way, it surely is great for getting more attention, which will really help your brand. Stay up to date with the topics, and participate in Twitter chats as much as you can. You can also promote your Twitter chats across your other social media platforms to drive your followers to Twitter or use TweetDeck, Twubs, or other similar tools for this purpose.

Strategy 2: Proper Hashtag Use

Everyone knows the importance of hashtags on Twitter. The majority of exploration and searching takes place due to the use of the right hashtags. However, beware; it can cause the complete opposite effect if misused. Depending on the type of brand or content, research the right hashtags or use tools that determine a certain set of hashtags to post with your content. This helps in marking your presence by grouping your content with relevant posts. This way, users can also search your profile easily.

There is also a rising trend of inventing your own hashtag and encouraging your followers to use it to increase interaction. For example, you can organize contests that enable your followers to tag other users with your invented hashtag, which has the potential of going viral and helping you get recognition.

Strategy 3: The Use of Visuals

Visual content has been proven to engage audiences three times more than simple text. Posting visual content shows thoughtfulness and adds personality to your account. Whether it is an image, video, or GIF, followers react more to visual content as it tends to deliver a clearer message and show effort.

Short Videos

Short videos are the truest form of engagement on any social media platform, and this obviously applies to Twitter as well. With the extensive use of smartphones, more people are turning to the mobile application of this platform and driving more than 90 percent of video views. You can either post an already-recorded video or experiment with different video lengths by filming a video directly from your smartphone. And because it plays automatically, your audience is instantly invested in this type of content as they scroll.

GIFs

GIFs are an underrated type of content that can make for powerful marketing action. They are much, much more than short, funny graphics, and can be used to convey robust information that will grab your audience's attention within a short period. You can also edit your visual content and compile cuts to highlight your products or other important information regarding your brand.

Images and Videos

To create visual content in the form of images and videos, you can use the following content ideas to create more engagement:

- Create a video series that rotates around "a typical day in the office" or behind the scenes.
- Interview all employees one by one and make it a weekly type of content.

- Hand over your account to an influencer to fetch more followers and give it a fresh twist.

- Include DIY projects or post "how-to" videos showing your products.

- Conduct quizzes and giveaway contests for more user interaction.

- Go for a crossover with other brands or companies, depending on the type and size of your brand.

- Put live video tweets to use, as mentioned above.

A Few More Tips

While these strategies are important to keep your marketing alive, there are certain things that you still need to pay attention to.

- *Building a Great Profile*

Now that your Twitter account is up and running, it is time to build your profile to create an impact on your followers and future audiences. Apart from writing a brilliant bio that captures the attention of potential followers, you also need to add specific keywords, your location, and certain hashtags that will strengthen your profile. You know you have succeeded in building a top-notch profile when your followers send you direct messages or congratulate you for your real-time presence. Also, you'll probably be gaining followers quickly.

Since this platform allows you to use fewer characters within your bio, you need to be smart in writing a catchy intro as it'll act as a first impression on your followers.

Make your brand seen by further tweaking your profile, using your location and SEO strategies. Also, try to get verified as soon as you can. Getting verified shows your users that you are authentic, and thus, they can trust your brand.

- *Delving into Analytics*

You can use Twitter analytics to measure and reveal statistics behind your account's engagement and followers. You can visualize the demographics of your content, followers, and location. You can also measure the interaction of your followers on every post, such as likes, comments, and retweets. This can give you a clearer picture of the type of content that generates more interaction, thus guiding you in the right direction.

- *Scheduling and Posting*

People are more active on social media, particularly on Twitter, during specific hours of the day. It is the peak time for engagement and the right time to post your content for maximum likes, comments, and retweets before your tweet gets lost in the world of oblivion. The most advisable times to tweet are 12 p.m., 5 p.m., and 6 p.m., but this can vary depending on the type of your followers and content.

How much you post per day matters, too. You need to tweet at least once a day to garner more attention. The more frequently you tweet, the more presence you gain. Try experimenting with different timings and varied frequency to achieve maximum engagement. Schedule your tweets and content accordingly, or use tools to predict the optimum time for posting, and automatically upload content.

Finally, remember to follow your marketing plan. Do not just schedule it and forget about it; be consistent and keep going. It is a slow start for everyone, but eventually, you will build a gigantic community as long as you stay consistent and original.

Chapter 10: Instagram Marketing

Instagram is one of the most popular social media platforms, with a total of more than 800 million users. What is striking about Instagram is that at least 500 million users are active daily, and the growth rate is staggering to the extent that there is an increase of 100 million users per month. This makes it an essential platform for any business to not only appear on but also spread awareness about their brand, driving traffic to their website and boosting their overall sales.

While Instagram users were initially known to be mostly composed of young people, making it extremely beneficial for businesses that target youth, the older generations are also embracing the platform and have started to make an appearance there, which makes it easier for you to reach various types of audiences.

Using Instagram is valuable to your business as the engagement rate on posts—a whopping 4.21 percent—is 58 times higher than Facebook and 120 times higher than Twitter. So, if you are looking to grow your business, reach a wider audience, and get the most ROI, here are three strategies you should be using on Instagram:

Strategy 1: Instagram Stories

One of the things that makes Instagram successful is that its team is always developing the platform and looking for ways to ensure that users will not only continue to use it but also stay longer. One of the features that they added was Instagram stories, and it has become an even more advantageous and useful tool for you to use. That is because 400 million users are scrolling through Instagram stories daily, making story ads an excellent way to reach a larger audience. So, how do you use Instagram stories to your advantage?

Story ads allow your business ad to show up between stories and reach users as they flick through other stories. But what is truly captivating about Instagram stories is that they give you the chance to be so much more fun and creative, as well as visually appealing. Story ads let your business use all the available Instagram story features to put together an ad that's captivating and interesting, or one that requires a user to become more interactive. Here are a few tips to help your business make the most of Instagram stories, especially since the click-through rate on stories is much higher than feed ads, making the return on investment even higher:

Create Fun and Interesting Content

You only have 15 seconds to get your message across and reach your audience, so you really need to make the most of it. However, with the tools available on Instagram stories, you can make your stories eye-catching and interesting. These tools include text overlay, which allows you to highlight the message you want to send and make it stand out—loud and clear. You can also use the GIFs that are installed in the story features, which are definitely funny and cute, and they have the power to captivate the audience with their playfulness.

Use Polls and Sliders

Another feature on Instagram stories that really helps build a relationship with the audience is the use of polls and sliders to get the audience to engage with your business profile. With polls, you can post an image and have users vote for the one they prefer by giving them the option of choosing left or right. You can also ask a question and have them respond by giving them options to vote or using an open-ended reply. However, in most cases, voting gets a higher response as it requires much less effort on the user's part. With sliders, you get the audience to engage just by using a sliding emoji to react to your story and show that they liked it. The reason these Instagram story features are a great form of content is that they require the target audience to engage with your post, which helps you build a warmer relationship with potential customers.

Build a Relationship with Your Audience

Because there are so many businesses out there, most users tend to appreciate getting up close and personal and seeing what happens behind the curtains. You can use Instagram stories to your advantage by allowing your audience to view the behind-the-scenes content. This could be done by showing the process of how your products come to life, taking their opinions on future designs, or even having them see the faces behind the brand and build a personal connection with it through witnessing day-to-day activities. This way, they get to know you and your employees on a personal level. Instagram stories allow you to be funny, unconventional, or personal, as the stories only last for 24 hours, which means you don't need to stick 100 percent to your polished and professional business persona.

Use Consumer-Generated Content

Instagram stories allow your business to get much more interactive with the audience, as many campaigns can be solely led on Instagram. This can be done by asking your audience to post a photo with your product in order to win a free product, show how they used it in a smart, funny, or silly way, or come up with an idea that encourages the user to post on your behalf, tagging your account and helping you reach their audience, too.

Other Tips

Apart from polls, sliders, and user-generated content, there are other ways to get your audience to engage with your stories. Here are a few tips for using this feature effectively:

- **Mentions**

Mentioning another account, user, or even an influencer in your stories is an easy way of getting them to re-post your content on their own stories. This means you get to reach a wider audience.

- **Highlights**

One of the updated features of Instagram allows you to save stories to your profile as highlights and displays them to other users when they first land on your page. This makes it easier to show them whatever it is that is important to you.

- **Geotags**

One of the Instagram story features that helps reach a specific audience is the use of geotags. They appeal to users of that specific area as they can connect more with your brand, and they can be viewed by people within that location even if they are not following you.

- **Hashtags**

Instagram is all about hashtags. Using one in your stories will automatically add it to the list of posts in that hashtag, helping your business become visible to new users and potential followers.

Strategy 2: Shopping Posts

For businesses that use Instagram as a tool to market their products, Instagram Shopping can really help boost sales. Instead of depending on your users having to head to your website, store, or even DM to ask for more information, Instagram Shopping allows them to make a purchase right then and there.

Why is Instagram Shopping a Great Marketing Tool?

- **Acts as a Virtual Store for Your Business**

With Instagram Shopping, you can now display the prices of your products whenever a user taps on the photo on your feed. To make it even easier for the users to make an instant purchase, they can tap on the price, select the size and color they want, and check out. This also increases the level of engagement on each post; the more people see them, the more taps you get.

- **Allows You to Redirect Traffic to Your Store**

If you do not want to use Instagram as your virtual store and are more interested in gaining more traffic on your website, you could easily redirect users to your store once they have clicked on the post on your feed, checked the price, and decided to make a purchase. Instagram Shopping allows you to add a link to your website or virtual store, and have people perform the transaction there, increasing the traffic on your web page through your Instagram account.

- **Gives Your Business Numerous Ways of Presenting Your Products**

You can choose to display your products in carousel shopping, allowing your business to present a variety of products at the same time due to the ability to tag 20 different products in the same post. This is a great advertising tool, as you can showcase an entire collection and reach more than one audience at a time, while still paying the bare minimum.

Another option is to use a feed post, where you can tag up to five products. This makes it possible for you to put together an entire outfit or display with products that complement each other. You can even post Instagram stories with the tagged products, giving you the ability to use them as story ads.

Setting up Instagram Shopping

If you already have an Instagram account for your business, it is pretty easy to set up Instagram Shopping:

- **Step 1: Make Sure Your Business Account Complies with Instagram Shopping Requirements**

Your business must be located in one of the 46 approved countries, such as the United States, Canada, Puerto Rico, France, United Kingdom, Germany, Italy, Spain, Netherlands, Sweden, Switzerland, Ireland, South Africa, Belgium, Austria, Poland, Greece, Portugal, and more.

Aside from that, you must have a business profile on Instagram and fulfill the requirements for Instagram's merchant agreement and commerce policy.

- **Step 2: Connect Your Instagram Account to a Facebook Catalog**

To set up a catalog of products on Instagram, you must have a Facebook page linked to your Instagram account, with a Facebook catalog displaying your products.

You can do this by going to your Facebook business page and adding a shop section. All you have to do is click on the Shop tab and follow these steps:

1. Press on Set up Shop and agree to the terms and conditions.

2. Enter the business address and click on Next.

3. Choose what currency you would like to use for your Facebook shop, then enter your business email address and click Next.

4. Add your tax registration info.

5. Once you have clicked Finish, you can begin adding products to your shop.

- **Step 3: Your Account will be Verified**

Instagram will then verify your account and check whether you comply with all the requirements before granting you access. It could take quite a while, so be patient.

- **Step 4: Add Product Tags to Your Posts**

Once Instagram has given you the green light and granted you access to Shopping, you can start tagging products on your posts just like you would tag people.

After choosing a photo from your gallery, editing the filters, and adding the captions and hashtags you want to include in your post, you will find a Tag Products option right beneath Tag People. Click on it and start typing the name of the product. Remember: You can tag up to five products in your post. Once you are done, you can share your post, and it will be added to your feed.

Strategy 3: Instagram Ads

With Instagram being so popular, it is a great tool for businesses to use for advertising purposes. It allows you to get much more creative and reach a wider audience, as well as ensuring a greater return on investment due to the high engagement rate, making it an extremely useful and cheap advertising tool. You can even include Instagram ads in your Facebook ad campaigns—it is easy and hassle-free. Here are a few ways through which you can get the optimum results when advertising on Instagram:

Video Ads

Video ads are the future of social media, and that is why it is essential to incorporate them into your advertising strategy. With 72 percent of posts shared on Instagram being photos, videos give your business a real advantage to stand out. However, when using them as an advertising tool, you need to ensure that your videos still have the visual appeal that fits the platform's identity. This can be done by introducing the video with colors and beautiful imagery—also, try to avoid being extremely promotional. To get the best results while using video ads, you should make the video short and captivating by keeping it fun or interesting. You can invoke a certain emotion, offer a quick tip, or a piece of advice.

Another tip when creating video ads is to use vertical videos, as they take up more of the screen space and allow your video to play automatically when someone is scrolling through their feed. This means the ideal video size for Instagram is 600x750 pixels. To grab the user's attention instantly, you need to get right to business and start your video with something appealing to stop the user from scrolling. Even though it is a promotional video, you need to avoid starting your video with a company logo or anything that looks too promotional, or else you will lose their attention right away. Remember that most people have their sound off, to begin with, so you need to use strong visuals to get them to put the sound back on.

GIFs or Boomerangs

Video content does not have to be produced and filmed—it can even be done by using animated GIFs of your products, or even one of your products prettified with an animated GIF tool that will add a bit of authenticity and character to it. Another great option is using Boomerang, which displays a playful movement on the screen, making your product appear so much more appealing. You can use the visuals of a customer using your product, unboxing it, or adding it to a relative environment. It is catchy, short, and will definitely stand out from a sea of photographs, making it a great way to reach your audience and use advertising on Instagram to your advantage.

Influencers

Whether you like the idea of influencers or not, they really help you reach a wider audience and raise awareness about your brand or products. There are so many different levels of influencers on Instagram, and not all of them come with an expensive rate card. You will find mid-range influencers who still have thousands of followers, but not hundreds of thousands or millions, making them a cheaper option.

The reason why collaborating with an influencer yields great results on Instagram is that they have a large fan base of people who look up to them, enjoy their content, and trust them enough to hear what they are saying. Due to the high level of engagement most influencers have, when they give your business a shout-out or mention it in their stories, posts, or short videos, you will most likely gain quite a few followers and let them know that your business exists. However, it is essential to pick the influencer you'll collaborate with carefully, as you want to make sure that the right audience will be targeted and that their image will not harm your business in any way.

Lead Ads

One of the advantages of using lead ads on Instagram is that they do not require the audience to exert much effort, but still allow you to build the first step of a customer relationship without being too promotional. This can be done by asking them to subscribe to your newsletter or receive a tip, freebie, or update via email. However, because Instagram already has all the necessary info stored, it doesn't require the users to fill in their details but displays the automated personal info a customer needs, only requiring them to click "submit".

Story Ads

As mentioned above, Instagram stories are gaining popularity, making them an excellent tool for advertising. While you can choose from many different types of story ads to display to your users, in general, an engaging story will probably perform better. This can be done through polls, sliders, lead ads, or getting users to swipe up and land on your web page. Just keep in mind that you only have 15 seconds to grab their attention, so your ad really needs to be captivating.

There are so many reasons a business needs to have a strong presence on Instagram. As it is a continuously growing platform, it makes for a great marketing tool for any business to use. Helping you reach your marketing goals, whether it is reaching a broader audience, boosting sales, or having a stronger online presence, Instagram is a tool that your business should be using.

Chapter 11: Snapchat Marketing

More than just an entertaining social media platform, Snapchat is extensively used for marketing these days. "But it's nothing more than filters and quirky lenses," you say? Well, brands are now starting to realize the potential of this underrated tool that has evolved over the years. The concept of disappearing images and videos was once considered as weak content that could not garner much interaction. Back then, creating a budget and investing in this platform seemed like a waste of time and money. However, with a lot of experiments and some notable experience spanning many years, this concept has turned out to be a powerful strategy for all brands who are trying to make their mark online.

Snapchat once witnessed a low point after its launch, but then escalated rapidly between the years 2015 and 2016, when users doubled from 100 million to 200 million worldwide. Around 75 percent of these users are active daily on Snapchat, spending around 25 to 30 minutes on the app every day. If your brand is targeting a younger audience, such as users in their early 20s and the Gen Z population, Snapchat is the right platform for you.

Why Snapchat?

A few astonishing stats revealed the power of this social media platform and how it could be a major tool for your business in driving more revenue and sales. As mentioned, Snapchat caters to over 200 million users who collectively watch more than 10 billion videos daily. While users watch this bewildering number of videos, they enthusiastically contribute to it and produce over 3 billion videos daily, 76 percent of which include online shopping products. Snapchat has recently overtaken other platforms like Twitter, LinkedIn, and Pinterest, with more registered users who are active regularly. A significant chunk of such users is based in the United States and North America.

Reasons to Include Snapchat in Your Marketing Plan

• **Provides a Different Kind of Engagement**
This book has discussed over and over again how stories, as a concept for engagement, have boomed. And that is what Snapchat is all about; images and videos that disappear after 24 hours. Users are bound to remember moving images and videos better than stationary text content. Stories provide you with the opportunity to form creative content that stays fresh and does not become repetitive. Your users will most likely not recall content that was posted a few months ago, which can be a major advantage. You can create campaigns or snippets of your long videos to offer your users a sneak peek of your next project, like Taco Bell has been doing for a while.

• **Ranks Among the Least Competitive Platforms**
As mentioned at the beginning of this chapter, Snapchat has been underestimated as a marketing platform. Many brands are still avoiding its use and turning to Instagram, Facebook, and Twitter. It is high time that you tapped into this platform and made the most of it.

Since a lot of brands and companies have yet to discover the potential of Snapchat for marketing, there is less competition there. It's the right time to establish your presence and create engagement through this platform.

- **Laid-Back**

If your company or business demands a rather professional and formal language for user engagement, Snapchat is not for you. However, this platform has given a certain personality to most of the brands that use it. With disappearing content, filters, lenses, doodles, real-time videos, and bitmojis, this medium is fresh, raw, and quirky, hence attracting a younger crowd. It doesn't pressure you or your brand into being more formal. In fact, it encourages you to be more open and interactive with your followers, showing them your brand's real face.

- **Tech-Driven**

Many social media platforms today use technologically updated features such as geolocations and augmented reality. Snapchat started it all. With new filters, lenses, and features that are updated every once in a while, within the app, Snapchat can be called a tech-savvy platform. This book has discussed the onset, importance, and future of augmented reality in the previous chapters, along with how users and potential followers can be lured in with this feature for effective marketing.

Strategy 1: Linked Stories

The "swipe up" feature in Snapchat has been handy since its introduction, especially for brands and companies who are trying to generate revenue through social media. You can now attach links of websites or apps to any story or snap that you send to your customers, and it has become one of the most powerful marketing strategies. Once your customers click on the "swipe up" link, they are directed to a new window that will either contain a relevant article or your website. Functioning rather as ads, the concept of linked stories will be discussed further in this chapter. But before that, first, understand the procedure of attaching links to your stories.

➢ Click on a relevant image or record a video based on your content requirement, or upload a picture from your gallery. Add filters, emojis, music, and stickers if you prefer.

➢ When you check the snap preview, you'll see an icon that represents linking websites and URLs.

➢ You'll get a Type a URL option. Copy and paste the URL of the website you want to link, or type it in if you remember. You can view this link in a window within the app.

➢ Next, you can find an Attach to Snap option at the bottom of the page. Tap it to link the website with your image or video. You can now send it to your friends or put it up as a story.

This helpful feature can also be used within chats. You just need to copy and paste the URLs in the chats or directly type them while replying to your friends. Even though this feature has been up and running since July 2017, not many companies are taking advantage of it. So, it is a good idea to link your stories directly with your company's shopping page or blog by creating compelling content to drive more sales and increase traffic.

Strategy 2: Behind-the-Scenes Snaps

This is, by far, the rawest form of engagement any brand can offer. By showing behind-the-scenes content to your followers, you increase your chances for interaction and engagement as they tend to trust you more. These exclusive peeks and insights into your office and employees will be highly appreciated by your audience. It is truly a delight to watch the making of people's favorite products, and the work put in by every member of your team. When your customers know and have access to everything that goes on in the backstage of your work, they can fully trust you by becoming familiar with your company's vibe and character.

How to Use Behind-the-Scenes Content on Snapchat

- ## A Day in your Office

Shoot an entire day at your workplace and highlight all the peak points in a regular workday that make it exciting. Begin by entering your office, having standard interactions and conversations with your colleagues as you normally would, and add a few glimpses of important moments.

- ## Employee Q&A

Let your entire team handle your brand's Snapchat account and conduct interviews among themselves—or any enthusiastic followers once you get a few. Include answers to questions like "Why do you like working here?" and "How has this brand become an integral part of your life?"

- ## How it's Made

If you have a factory or a workshop that manufactures your products, take your followers on a virtual tour to show them how your products are made. This will showcase the true quality of your products and prove to your customers that you are not afraid to show them the process.

- ## Humor and Fun

If your team consists of hilarious people, you can conduct a few pranks or riddle quizzes among them, or simply create funny content to keep your audience thoroughly engaged. Funny content is bound to spread and be shared more often, keeping your customers and followers waiting for more.

Strategy 3: Snapchat Ads

Snapchat Ads is a new feature designed for marketers and content creators, and it is a raging success. This new update has allowed brands and companies to reach millions of users worldwide and create brand awareness. Whether you need to drive sales or increase traffic on your website and social media platforms, Snapchat Ads cater to all purposes. This feature allows users to visit your website directly or drive local followers and users to your store. It also leads them to download your app by creating a path toward the Play Store or App Store.

You can sandwich your ads between your stories after carefully planning a day's content or any campaign. By showing your followers your intent and purpose, you can get them interested in swiping up the link on the ad. As mentioned, you can direct them to your website, online store, app, AR lens, or video to increase interaction and engagement.

Types of Ads

Snapchat offers a lot of advertisement options that are super effective in increasing followers and engagement. Depending on your brand and the content you create, the following features or ad types can be used to promote your products or services flawlessly.

- **Collection Ads**

Mainly useful for shopping and driving sales, Collection Ads allow you to show a range of products that can be viewed with simple taps and bought easily through a swipe-up link to your website or online store.

- **Snap Ads**

Consisting of a single image or video, Snap Ads provides you with the layout of an image, video, or GIF that lets users access your brand's website or app's link with just a single swipe.

- **Story Ads**

This feature displays your ad in the form of a "Discover" tile with other popular and trending ads and stories on your users' feeds. This targets your potential users based on the relevant demographics.

- **Filters and Lenses**

You can now create your own filters and lenses, and customize them to your brand's image. It is an impeccable way to generate interaction with your users through augmented reality and playful filters.

- **Non-Skippable Videos or Commercials**

Similar to Instagram and Facebook, you can also create non-skippable, commercial-quality video content to serve as ads for your brand. You can place them among your premium, widespread content,

Snapchat Ads Manager

With the business version of Snapchat, you can create ads on the go. This social media platform has created Ads Manager, which is a self-serve tool to create ads. It gives you the flexibility to create an amazing image and video content and manage your ads at absolutely no cost. Once you have your account set up on Ads Manager, you are good to go. Not only can you create content and plan your campaigns through this free tool, but you can also choose your audience depending on your location, and analyze the performance of your ads.

In the Ads Manager window, you can access the Dashboard and Creative Library keys to create, edit, and view your ads. The Custom Audiences option allows you to choose and target your audience depending on your brand, location, and other demographics. Lastly, the Help Center helps you navigate your way through Ads Manager and guides you through common issues.

Take a look at the way Ads Manager works and some necessary steps to take:

1. First, identify the main objective behind your ad or campaign—whether it is to generate more leads, increase followers, or just spread brand awareness.

2. Set a start and end date with a proper schedule for your ad, in addition to choosing a name.

3. Depending on the age, gender, location, language, demographics, and type of followers, define your target audience using the available options.

4. Next, set a budget, the minimum being $100. This allows Snapchat to show your ads to users who are interested in your business and likely to buy your products or install your app.

5. Choose your snap-type from the options Top Snap Only, Web View, App Install, and Long Form Video. Create your headline, write your brand name, and finally, select your call-to-action option.

After you have launched your ad, you can monitor its performance through the ad metrics feature. It notifies you of your campaign's reach, the money spent, and the impressions it has made. It is highly recommended that you use Ads Manager if you are planning on using Snapchat as your marketing platform.

Additional Tips

These three strategies can become major guiding principles for your Snapchat marketing plan. However, to make it even better, you need to follow these important tips:

Don't Cross-Post

While people know that Instagram and Facebook copied Snapchat's original concept of posting content through stories, it still holds its authentic authority. However, a few brands cross-post the same content on Snapchat, Instagram, Facebook, and Twitter, over and over again. At some point, it gets monotonous and boring. If you do this, you could end up losing many followers on all your social media platforms, which could be risky for your brand, especially if you are running a business online.

Plan your content differently for all the social media platforms you are using, and try not to be repetitive. You might run out of ideas sometimes, and cross-posting once in a while is still okay. But doing it regularly is a big no-no. Keep your content diverse but follow your brand's language. It will make your followers curious and urge them to follow your brand on every social media platform to know what is cooking.

Reach the Right Audience

At times, even if you sell products that are efficient and show a lot of potentials, you can fail to drive sales and generate the targeted revenue over a specific period. You might also be on the right track when it comes to social media marketing. So, what could be wrong? A major factor that could disrupt your interaction with followers—and lead to poor sales—might be your business's inability to reach the relevant audience. You need to reach the accessible Snapchatters that would genuinely be interested in your products.

You can target users based on their age, household income, gender, likes and dislikes, habits, country, and city. Snapchat offers you some amazing tools to identify and target your potential customers, which could completely change your social media marketing game and generate more sales.

Like other social media platforms, Snapchat can also be intimidating at first. You just need to remain patient and be consistent to establish your brand's presence and create spectacular engagement. Now that you have read about various social media platforms in detail, it is time to build on this information and formulate your marketing plan. However, before you get to that, keep reading to learn more about influencer marketing and the top tools you can use this year to polish your marketing strategies, as well as the future of social media marketing to help you stay ahead of the game.

Chapter 12: The Rise of Influencer Marketing and How to Use It

Influencer marketing is a great marketing tool for your business due to its extreme effectiveness. Not only have 86 percent of marketers been actively using influencer marketing, but also the number of Google searches for "influencer marketing" has increased by 1,500 percent over the past three years.

The reason why influencer marketing has become imperative for businesses to include in their marketing strategies is that influencers on social media help you reach your specific target audience and increase their awareness of your brand. That is because social media influencers have a large following, as well as a strong connection and relationship with their fan base. This makes your target audience reliable, loyal, and willing to accept and follow the advice of their role models.

Why Is Influencer Marketing on the Rise?

Celebrity marketing has been used for decades, where a celebrity would endorse a certain brand, becoming the brand's image or being seen using its products. However, using a celebrity is not only a costly method of advertising but also not quite as effective—since most people are aware of the fact that it is a marketing strategy.

Nowadays, with social media giving regular customers a voice, it has enabled people who are interested in a specific sector to get more recognition because of their authenticity and awareness. As people with the same interests start to follow their journeys, the number of their followers increase, turning them into an influencer. Because they are real-life customers who offer authentic and valuable information and reviews to their followers, they are considered role models who have the power to affect the choices their followers make. Based on statistics provided by Mediakix, 80 percent of marketers agree that influencer marketing is effective, and 71 percent also conclude that the customers generated by influencer marketing are of excellent quality.

As a marketer, using influencers to help promote a business is an excellent way to reach an audience that is not only interested in what your business offers, but will also become potential buyers, leading to a boost in sales and revenue. That is because the fan base of influencers usually consists of those who share an interest in the niche market that you are part of, and they tend to follow these influencers to gain more knowledge about that sector. The difference between influencers and celebrities is that the level of trust, loyalty, and engagement on an influencer's social media platforms is so much higher, making the ROI and outcome of influencer marketing much more beneficial for your business.

How Does a Business Use Influencer Marketing?

There are numerous influencers available for every sector you can think of. You will find travel, fashion, food, lifestyle, and beauty influencers; vloggers and bloggers; advocates for human rights, LGBTQ+ rights, and gender equality; as well as people who fight for any other social or environmental cause, and many others.

So, the first thing businesses should do is figure out who the influencers in their sectors are. This can be done by checking your followers, as you might find that some of your customers are influencers who believe in your brand and what you have to offer. You can also analyze the other people your fans follow and pinpoint whom they find to be influential.

Once you have identified the best influencers to use, then you have two options: try to reach out to them on their social media platforms, or contact an agency and have them give you access to the influencers.

What Can an Influencer Do for Your Business?

The advantage of working with niche influencers is that it generates the exact type of target audience you are looking for—the people who are most likely to become potential customers. All you have to do is choose the type of influencer who is in line with your brand and relevant to your niche market.

In fact, many businesses tend to use influencer marketing to raise awareness about their brands. Statistics show that 37 percent of marketers have admitted to using influencer marketing to build brand awareness because of how effective it is, but that is not the only reason. Here are several other ways your business can benefit from working with influencers:

Review Your Products or Services

One of the most common ways of using an influencer is by sending them a product to use or having them try out your services firsthand. Afterward, they give their honest opinion and offer reviews about their experience with your brand. This helps your business gain more potential customers, as working with a niche influencer gives you access to the right target audience.

Give your Business a Shout-Out

Whether it is through a post, short video, or even stories, an influencer giving your business a shout-out will help their fan base get familiar with what your brand has to offer. This can be a great way to generate more targeted followers.

Take Over Your Account

Another way of using an influencer for marketing purposes is by carrying out a social media take-over. The influencer will have access to your account and interact with your audience directly. This way, your followers can ask questions, and the influencer will answer them, offering them insight into their day and giving them a chance to connect with a person they look up to. Because influencers tend to announce on their social media platforms that they will be taking over your account, you'll find their followers also heading to your account, bringing you more traffic and engagement, and spreading awareness about your products or services.

Collaboration

You can choose to collaborate with an influencer by having them announce your latest campaigns, give their followers a discount code for your products, or even become a brand ambassador for your business. All these can really help boost sales, as their fan base will have a lot of faith and trust in the influencer's recommendations.

Create Content

Many people tend to use influencers because they are great at creating authentic and real video content that appeals to the consumer. Instead of spending large sums of money on professional video production, you can spend a fraction of that price on hiring an influencer who will create engaging content for your brand. That way, you will ensure that the engagement level will be extremely high, as they have their family, friends, and followers to vouch for them.

Micro-Influencers vs. Celebrity Influencers: Which Type of Influencer Is Best for Your Business?

When it comes to influencers, there is always the dilemma of which type to use. There are celebrity influencers who have hundreds of thousands of followers and sometimes even millions, whereas micro-influencers have thousands or tens of thousands of followers. So, how do you choose which one is better for your business?

The number of followers is not always the most important factor you should be analyzing; instead, you should be looking at the engagement rate to help you decide. In most cases, you will find that the more followers an influencer gets, the less engagement they have, indicating that more followers don't always mean more interaction.

On the contrary, since niche fans are aware of the identity of their influencers and choose whom they want to support and look up to, they tend to have more faith and loyalty in smaller-sized influencers. They feel they can relate to them and trust their judgment. Most people know that the bigger the fan base, the more an influencer is approached by brands, making them lose their credibility and authenticity in the long run.

Benefitting from Micro-Influencers

Here are a few reasons why instead of opting for a few celebrity influencers, you should use ten to 20 micro-influencers:

- **Higher Engagement Rates**

HelloSociety has found that micro-influencers or accounts with 30,000 or fewer followers are much more beneficial to marketers. That is because these influencers tend to deliver 60 percent higher engagement rates as their fan base is smaller, more engaged, and more loyal.

- **Cost-Effective**

One of the advantages of using influencer marketing is that it is incredibly cost-effective. In fact, influencers are 6.7 times more cost-effective than celebrities, and they create 22 times as much buzz. This means that every dime you are paying is worth it, and the return on investment is really high.

- **Cheaper**

Because micro-influencers are much cheaper, they allow your business to use several influencers at the same cost as using one or two celebrity influencers. This gives you the advantage of reaching a wider, more precise audience that will really help grow your business more effectively.

- **Diverse Content**

Using several micro-influencers allows you to get creative with your business and try out different strategies to see which resonates best with the audience. That not only makes your brand look creative and innovative but also offers the user a variety of content to choose from, as well as catering to different audiences. For example, you can ask one influencer to post on their social media platforms, another one to get their audience to take part in a campaign, a third one to create video content, and a fourth one to review or test out your products. This will allow you to have interesting and engaging content, in addition to making your brand look like it is super exposed and popular among most of the influencers in that niche.

- **Easier to Reach and Communicate With**

Most micro-influencers will respond to your inquiries via social media, instead of you having to hire an agency to get through to them. They are also less picky and more open to several suggestions, making them much easier to deal with.

- **Higher ROI**

As mentioned above, because of the power influencers have over their audience, they can direct them to your business and products, convincing them to test them out. This means that every dime you spend on influencer marketing comes with a higher ROI, making it a great marketing tactic to use.

If you are wondering whether your business should be working with influencers, then the answer is definitely "Yes!" Not only is the rise in influencer marketing growing, but it is also extremely effective, powerful, and helpful when it comes to reaching the precise audience you need for your business to grow. However, you need to choose the influencers carefully by analyzing their content, followers, and personalities to make sure that they are relevant to your brand and comply with its identity. Working with influencers will also help you produce creative content that will appeal to your consumers and really tap into different audiences, which will grow your social media presence, boost your sales, increase your followers, and provide you with loyal customers who believe in your brand and what you have to offer.

Chapter 13: Top 7 Social Media Tools for 2020

Growing your social media organically is not an easy task, but it is not impossible either. With the right tools and a good understanding of the different data you can make use of, you can really optimize your content to be more visible, sought-after, and useful for your target audience. In order for you to do this, here are some useful tools for organic growth that you can explore in 2020:

1. TubeBuddy

Because video content is a key focus in 2020, you should be ensuring that you are stepping up your game on YouTube and focusing on video content that is useful, highly searchable, and appealing to a wide audience. That is where TubeBuddy comes in; it gives your business a competitive edge when you're trying to figure out what type of content to create and optimizing your video to make sure that it ranks highly on the search tabs. If you're new to TubeBuddy, you'll find that there's a free version and paid version. Once you've downloaded TubeBuddy, you can choose which one works best for you by skimming through the available features, but it is always a good idea to test the free version first and make sure you're comfortable with it before you go all in. For the most part, the free version still allows you to make use of many important features, such as the following:

Worthy Content Creation

One of the main advantages of using TubeBuddy is that it helps you find content that is searchable and optimizes your keywords for SEO purposes. Say that you are in the fitness industry and are wondering what type of content you should be putting out there. Naturally, the first thing that would come to mind is something about weight loss. To check whether this is a topic worth pursuing, you can add it to the search bar on TubeBuddy, and you will be presented with a keyword score that gives you the answer. This depends on the search volume, determining whether it is a topic that's widely searched, as well as the amount of competition available in terms of the existing content on that topic.

When the topic is highly searched and included in a lot of content that has already been created, it will be difficult for your video to rank high and get the recognition it deserves—in that case, that topic is not worth pursuing. However, TubeBuddy also provides you with related searches to give you other topic ideas. For example, one of the ideas that show up in related searches is "How to lose weight fast without exercise". When checking the keyword score, it changes from poor to good because it is highly searched, but there is not as much content available on this specific topic, making it an option you could consider. This helps you understand that the content you will create will rank high and be visible to your audience, too. You don't just want to create content that is highly searched; you also want it to be visible on the first page of search results so that people can find it easily. That's how you decide whether it's worth it or not.

Keyword Research

TubeBuddy also allows you to find out what keywords a competitor's video includes through tags. This way, you can get a better understanding of your own keywords and how to optimize them to make your video more visible and searchable.

If you look at a successful video with over one million views, TubeBuddy does not just show you the keywords but also how the video ranks for each keyword. The reason why it's helpful is that it will inspire you to target better keywords by looking at what your competitors are using. You will see what's working for them and ensure that you are optimizing your keywords to make them more visible and rank higher on YouTube.

2. Keywords Everywhere

Keywords Everywhere is a Google plug-in extension that is a great tool for SEO optimization. It helps you with keyword research and is beneficial when it comes to content creation. It gives you content ideas based on the most popular searches.

Say that you work in sustainable fashion and want to create content around that topic. If you were to insert that keyword, Keyword Everywhere would give you insight into how many times a month this keyword has been searched, to help you decide whether it is worth creating content with it. This tool also gives you related keywords and other content that people who searched for sustainable fashion could be interested in, based on their searches. Having this insight really helps you understand the user, their interests, and what would make for beneficial content to use. By using it, you can create data-driven content that is searchable and ensure that your content is useful and visible to the audience.

3. Flume

If you are looking for a tool to make Instagram much more flexible for your business needs, then Flume is one you should consider. It allows you to reply to DMs straight from your computer to up your DM game on Instagram and stay on track of customer interaction. Through the conversations featured on Flume, you can respond to your DMs and quickly filter them. You can view the unread messages only, and be sure to respond to all those you haven't replied to yet.

You can also search for hashtags to understand how significant they are and decide which ones to include in your posts. By optimizing your posts this way, you will be making them visible to a broader audience. Flume will also make it much easier for you to create a connection with your followers, stay on top of your game, and respond to DMs promptly.

4. Later

Another Instagram tool you should consider using is Later. This tool allows you to plan your feed, schedule your posts, and auto-publish, so you do not have to worry about posting each one separately. You can automatically tag people in your posts, meaning that you don't have to be glued to your phone to use Instagram. It will allow you to pre-plan and schedule your content while using Instagram to your advantage.

Comment Features

The paid version of Later also allows you to reply to comments on your computer, making it easier and faster to connect with your audience. This is important because the latest Instagram algorithm requires you to be active in the comments section. The more comments you receive and write, the more reach your posts get. This, in turn, increases your chances of being visible on other people's feeds and getting a higher rate of engagement on your posts.

The tool also shows you all the comments that you have received on different posts to allow you to respond to them quickly, which will be beneficial in terms of growing faster and building a better relationship with your audience.

Instagram Analytics Tool

With Later's Instagram Analytics tool, you can get an overview of how your account is doing and monitor your analytics through useful graphs. Sure, you can use Instagram's own analytics tool for this purpose as well, but the audience analytics on Later offer more details that can be very helpful to your business. That is because these can aid you in figuring out what the best days and times to post are, leading to more engagement on your posts. This tool can even tell you the specific hour when you have the most followers online, so you can post at that time and maximize your engagement.

Looking at your demographics and seeing the breakdown of your audience will give you a better understanding of how many users you have in each country—instead of just the top five—as well as the main languages they speak. This can help you decide what language to use in your posts when targeting a specific audience.

Hashtag Features

You can follow hashtags on Later to help you repost trending content on specific topics, just by clicking on them and adding them to your library to post later.

If you are looking to schedule your stories and find hashtags, you will also be able to do that on Later. You can click on hashtag suggestions, enter a keyword, and be given a list of popular hashtags that are relevant to this keyword.

5. Your Analytics

One of the key tools you should be using this year is your very own analytics. Each platform has its own analytics tool to help you get a better understanding of how your posts are performing. They also provide you with detailed insight into your audience so that you can optimize your content accordingly. On Instagram, for example, if you head to View Insights and swipe up, you will see even more data that is collected by Instagram. You can learn about how people found your post, and whether they are following you or not, you can get an idea of where they're coming from, and also determine whether your hashtag strategy is on point or not. If many people are not actually following you or found you through your hashtags, it is a great indication that your hashtags are optimized.

Another advantage of using analytics is that it helps you analyze your content and see how each post has performed. You can get an understanding of your reach per post, how many profile visits and likes you got, what your level of engagement is, etc. This helps you understand what kind of content has been more successful and engaging, giving you an idea of what is working for your brand. Getting an overview of other things like the number of saves and website clicks, as well as which posts made people visit your profile or generated website clicks, will also be beneficial to gain perspective on what kind of content works best for your audience.

6. Anchor

While video content is here to stay, many people are also heading toward audio content, as they are not always available to sit down and watch a video. That is why podcasts are becoming extremely popular, and they are one of the channels your business should focus on this year. The anchor is the tool you should be using to figure out how to use podcasts and have an all-in-one solution to get you started, as well as get distribution to iTunes and Spotify. Voice marketing is set to be huge in 2020, and it's a key strategy you can use to reach a wider audience.

7. Quora

If you are a content-based business, then Quora is an essential tool you should capitalize on to help you understand what people are asking questions about in your niche. It also helps you identify yourself and your business as a leader in the field by answering these questions. Not only that, but you can take those answers and turn them into immediate content by posting them on your blog, or creating a video about them. Quora will give you fresh ideas on content creation, as well as ensuring that you're tackling issues that people are curious about.

Using these tools to your business's advantage will be an extremely effective move. They will allow you to make use of important data and create content that is visible and optimized. This way, your content will rank high and reach a broader audience, making your business grow organically, and fast.

Chapter 14: The Future of Social Media Marketing

Social media is constantly changing; just when you think you have got it all figured out, the platforms update their algorithms, and you are back to square one. That is why you must stay up to date, always be on the lookout for new pieces of information you can implement, and be willing to test out new strategies and tactics to ensure that your social media platforms are not outdated. To help you do that, here are some tips you can implement to keep up with the times:

Focus on User Engagement

On any given day, your posts on social media will most likely reach 1 percent of your followers. While that does sound like a tiny number, you can change your perspective and try to capitalize on that 1 percent. If you start keeping an eye on who actually reads your posts and interacts with them regularly, you can build on that and form a strong relationship with them. As a business, you can do this by always replying to their comments, or even reaching out and giving them a discount because they are considered to be loyal customers. Building relationships and engaging with your users on a personal level is the future of social media, and that is what will differentiate you from AI, which will not tailor feedback and responses to suit different people's reactions and characteristics. Using this tactic is an excellent way to turn those clicks and interactions into conversions.

Build Relationships

Another form of user engagement that is essential to the present and the future of social media marketing is creating content that will truly connect the user to your brand rather than focus on being promotional. Nobody goes on social media to be sold stuff, and that is why your content must focus on building relationships rather than selling products. The stronger the bond, the higher the possibility of conversion, but it's important to focus on creating that bond in the first place. If you create content that is useful, emotional, or funny without the intent of selling, a user is more prone to like, comment, or share your posts, allowing your content to reach a wider audience.

However, it is also useful to understand that a post can go viral based on the real comments that are visible on it. It's not just about likes or shares; the greatest strength lies in comments that go back and forth. That is why it's important always to give the users something to respond to in order to keep the conversation flowing. The more comments a post receives, the more likely it is that Facebook or Instagram will show the post to other people. But that's not the only benefit—once again, you will also be building a relationship in the process and making users feel more connected to your brand.

Create Your Own Influencers

While influencer marketing is still on the rise, its success might be temporary. That is why, as a business, you need to be prepared to have your own influencers. This means that you need to look into your own network, figure out who has influence, and use them to your advantage. Your employees, followers, and even your CEO might have some power that you should be using. The more connected to the brand a person is, the more power they will have when it comes to reaching the audience. Instead of looking for people with a high following, start looking for those within your network who are continually on social media, have the skill of building virtual relationships and engaging with their followers, and use them as the face and voice of the company. Users want to feel an individual connection to a business, and that's why personal branding is a huge and successful field that companies need to tap into from a different perspective. Utilizing the voice of those within your company—and who are familiar with your brand—will add a whole lot of authenticity to your business, instead of using the same strategies and tactics that everyone else is using.

Capitalize on Omnichannel Marketing

It is not enough to be on one platform anymore. To increase your rating and traffic, you need to be sharing to different platforms, targeting different audiences, and directing them to your websites. The more traffic you have, the higher the possibility of conversion rates, making it much more beneficial for a business. However, it is not smart to re-share content on different channels, especially when the content does not fit the identity and strategy of a specific platform. For example, if you want to spread an article, sharing it on your Instagram account with a screenshot of the headline will be quite pointless, as the user will not put effort into searching for the title. However, if you share it on your stories with a swipe-up link, it might be useful. You will realize that going for omnichannel marketing will make your cost-per-click go down, as it helps improve your numbers on all platforms.

Concentrate on Content Marketing

While many people have actually stopped reading, having your own content on your blog or website is still extremely advantageous, and is likely to stay that way in the future. That is because the content will redirect users to your products, and it can be used as a tool to generate conversions through search engine optimization. You can use more than one advertising tool to suit different kinds of people through Google ads, Facebook ads, and SEO.

Content will also allow you to tap into different markets that are underused and help you reap many benefits, such as translations. Instead of creating new content, your business can decide to target a different audience by translating the existing content into a language that does not involve as much competition as English. That way, you will make use of the people searching for this information, who will get familiar with what you have to offer just because they do not have enough resources available in their own language. Tapping into a market with a strong audience will enable you to dominate it quickly, maintain stability for a long while, and generate more revenue.

Use User Metrics to Beat Google

There is probably a lot of content that your business put out there without much of an outcome. Instead of throwing it away and deeming it useless, you can try and beat Google by playing by its own rules. In most cases, you will find that the reason why your posts did not perform well was that they weren't optimized with the necessary keywords to be visible on Google. And what does that mean? It means you have the opportunity to transform useless content into winning content just by making a few changes.

All you have to do is look for keywords that have less than a 5 percent click-through rate, and pages that have less than a 4 percent click-through rate and make sure that the keywords that you rank for are in the title tag as well as within the actual content. Once you make those changes, you'll have Google recrawl your site, and your click-through rate will skyrocket. To have the upper hand, you should be using list-related numbers and keywords such as "how-to, free, you, tips, blog post, why, best, tricks, and great". The next step is to wait for a month until Google has the chance to spread your posts to those searching for them, and then you'll see amazing results. Understanding the user and what they are searching for is the key to winning on all platforms.

Remember the Importance of Branding

Branding is not just used to identify your products or services, but it is beneficial to help you grow your brand for marketing purposes. That is because the bigger your brand, the more likely your content is to go viral. To cut down on fake news, most social media platforms determine authenticity based on size. So, when you have a larger number of followers, your content is more likely to be real, making it more visible than that of smaller companies in the same market. That's why focusing on growing your brand and social media presence with engaging content—without the sole intent of selling—will help your numbers grow, as the audience will get more interested in your content. There are also several tools you can use to grow your brand, which seems to be here to stay in the future, such as email marketing, push notifications, or a combination of both.

Don't Restrict Yourself to Conventional Traffic Methods

While pop-ups, quizzes, and newsletters are still useful for a business, they are not enough to help you stay ahead of the game. Look around you, and you will notice that because everyone is using these tactics, they are no longer effective. To stand out and offer something different and more powerful, you need to provide each user with a personalized experience.

The future of social media marketing is all about personalization. Your value as a marketer will lie in your ability to offer a personalized experience, as you'll be able to read different users and adapt to each one separately. While there are many data analysis tools out there, most of them do not factor in human differences—doing this will give you an advantage over the automated systems that are swooping up the market and trying to take your place. One of the most useful tools you'll have at hand is chats. Being able to speak to a customer, build a connection, and adapt to what they need will most likely translate into a conversion. In fact, the chat is now responsible for 28 percent of sales, and that's why the more personalization and authenticity you provide, the higher your conversion rates will be.

Think Like a Winner

Looking at some of the most successful people in the world, you will realize that the reason why they reached their true potential is that they had someone to guide them along the way—also, they never gave up. It is not enough to follow the trends because they are constantly changing. To become successful, you need to think like a winner and always be willing to acquire new information, test out different formulas, and be open to new ideas that could keep you on top. While some of them may not be useful, you just might find yourself setting a new trend and capitalizing on it before anyone else comes on board and reaps the benefits. Besides, you don't have to spend a fortune to gain new knowledge; there is a lot of free information available, just waiting for you to benefit from it.

You need to face the reality that marketing never stops. What works today won't necessarily work tomorrow, and the best approach is always to keep testing and learning in order to be prepared for the future. You will likely be bombarded with a whole lot of information, which will probably overwhelm you, but as long as you try one new thing at a time, you'll always be part of the change.

Conclusion

Thank you for making it to the end of this book. It should have been informative and provided you with all of the tools you need to achieve your goals.

The next step is to implement the important lessons, tips, and advice you learned. Remember that gaining knowledge is the most crucial step in setting up your business. However, it is how you apply what you have learned that will determine whether you will be successful.

Therefore, keep on learning, consult with your peers in the industry, watch for new developments, and always remain observant and positive.

Good luck with promoting your business in the world of social media!

Finally, if you found this book useful in any way, a review on Amazon is always appreciated.

Resources

https://www.contentfac.com/9-reasons-social-media-marketing-should-top-your-to-do-list/

https://www.oberlo.com/blog/social-media-marketing-statisticsht

https://www.smartinsights.com/social-media-marketing/social-media-strategy/new-global-social-media-research/

https://www.business2community.com/social-media/where-social-media-is-headed-in-2020-02266862

https://influencermarketinghub.com/social-media-trends/

https://www.socialmediatoday.com/news/6-key-social-media-trends-to-watch-in-2020/568481/

https://www.entrepreneur.com/article/343863

https://www.business2community.com/social-media/social-media-marketing-how-to-create-a-strong-personal-brand-02250816

https://thenextscoop.com/amazing-tips-help-personal-brand-grow-social-media/

https://blog.hootsuite.com/target-market/

https://promorepublic.com/en/blog/10-ways-find-audience-social-media/

https://devrix.com/tutorial/tips-grow-audience-stand-out-social-media/

https://www.lyfemarketing.com/blog/best-social-media-platforms/

https://buffer.com/library/social-media-sites
https://blog.hootsuite.com/how-to-advertise-on-facebook/
https://www.unboxsocial.com/blog/youtube-marketing-strategy2020/
https://www.youtube.com/watch?v=H3sIHuMMZec
https://www.youtube.com/watch?v=Ysm6CjDuKHs
https://digitalagencynetwork.com/best-twitter-marketing-strategies-to-use-in-2019/
https://blog.hootsuite.com/twitter-marketing/
https://coschedule.com/blog/how-to-use-instagram-stories/
https://later.com/blog/instagram-shopping/
https://www.youtube.com/watch?v=Q_xz4FMlljs
https://moosend.com/blog/snapchat-for-business/
https://www.lsb.com/blog/snapchat-clickable-links/
https://www.entrepreneur.com/article/338115
https://shanebarker.com/blog/rise-of-influencer-marketing/
https://www.youtube.com/watch?v=popowMuKyjY
https://www.youtube.com/watch?v=vqd2pzP5cjw
https://www.youtube.com/watch?v=3frb1JFzEKE
https://www.netbase.com/blog/social-media-tools-2020/
Neil Patel: https://www.youtube.com/watch?v=bGQG_-OG6fs
Carlos Gil: https://www.youtube.com/watch?v=apmIEnJIOm8
Frazer Brookes: https://www.youtube.com/watch?v=LL5b4p3TXL8

Printed in the USA
CPSIA information can be obtained
at www.ICGtesting.com
LVHW082035041123
762998LV00006B/537